THE HEADMASTER

BY JOHN MCPHEE

Looking for a Ship
The Control of Nature
Rising from the Plains
Table of Contents
La Place de la Concorde Suisse
In Suspect Terrain
Basin and Range
Giving Good Weight
Coming into the Country
The Survival of the Bark Canoe
Pieces of the Frame
The Curve of Binding Energy
The Deltoid Pumpkin Seed
Encounters with the Archdruid
The Crofter and the Laird
Levels of the Game
A Roomful of Hovings
The Pine Barrens
Oranges
The Headmaster
A Sense of Where You Are

The Headmaster
Frank L. Boyden, of Deerfield

by John McPhee

Macfarlane Walter & Ross

Toronto

First published by Farrar, Straus & Giroux

First published by Macfarlane Walter & Ross
in Canada in 1992

Macfarlane Walter & Ross
37A Hazelton Avenue
Toronto, Canada M5R 2E3

Canadian Cataloguing in Publication Data
McPhee, John, 1931–
The headmaster : Frank L. Boyden of Deerfield
1st Canadian ed.
ISBN 0-921912-41-2
1. Boyden, Frank Learoyd, 1879–1972.   2. Deerfield
Academy.   3. School principals—Massachusetts—
Deerfield—Biography.   I. Title.
LD7501.D43M26 1992   373.12'012'092   C92-094733-6

Except for the Preface and the illustrations, the contents
of this book appeared originally in The New Yorker and were
developed with the editorial counsel of William Shawn.

The section of photographs was drawn from a collection assembled
by Robert Crow, of Deerfield, Massachusetts. The chapter-end
sketches were done in 1943 by Donald Greason.

Design: Betty Crumley

Printed in the United States

To Robert McGlynn

Preface

This book was written in late 1965 and early 1966, and was first published in March of 1966 by *The New Yorker*. As a short biography, perhaps a third as long as a conventional biography might be, it has its own form, and is, actually, a kind of portrait, done at a specific time and from the vantage point of that time. I hope the reader will have a sense that he is looking at a picture of Frank L. Boyden, headmaster of Deerfield Academy, as he was soon after his eighty-sixth birthday, with details of his life and the history of his school coming in as elements in the portrait. Much of the story, particularly of the last and longest chapter, is written in the present tense, and I think that it should remain that way; for, more than anything else, it is the headmaster's immediacy that I have tried to arrest and to re-create.

John McPhee

Princeton, New Jersey

THE HEADMASTER

WHEN FRANK LEAROYD BOYDEN, who was soon to become the new headmaster of Deerfield Academy, arrived at the Deerfield station, he was only twenty-two. He walked downhill into the town for the first time, and he nodded, as he moved along, to women in full-length skirts, girls in petticoats, and little boys wearing long-sleeved shirts and bowler hats. Deerfield, Massachusetts, was essentially one street—a mile from the north to the south end—under shade so deep that even in the middle of the day the braided tracery of wagon ruts became lost in shadow a hundred yards from an observer. Twenty years would pass before the street would be paved, six years before it would be strung overhead with electric wires. Houses that had been built two hundred years earlier were the homes of farmers. Some of them tilted a little, and shingles were flaking off their roofs. Though the town was reasonably prosperous, much of it seemed slightly out of plumb. Deerfield Academy, the community's public school, was a dispiriting red brick building that appeared to have been designed to exclude as much sunlight as possible. A century earlier, there had been more than a hundred students in the academy, but now only fourteen boys and girls were enrolled for the approaching year, two of whom would constitute the senior class.

In one way, this decline was not discouraging to Boyden. He wanted to put Deerfield behind him as quickly as he could, for he wanted to go to law school and eventually to enter politics. He had been graduated from Amherst two months before. He knew that the people of Deerfield had offered the headmastership to other members of his class, but he was confident that he would get the job, because he was the only person who had applied. He had no money. Deerfield would pay eight hundred dollars a year. To save enough for law school, he intended to put away nearly every cent. He knocked at the door of a white frame house that belonged to Ephraim Williams, a trustee of the academy and the great-great-grandnephew of the founder of Williams College. "Mr. Williams," he said, "I'm Frank Boyden."

[4]

The day was Tuesday, August 12, 1902. The temperature outside was in the high eighties. But Ephraim Williams, a retired cavalry officer with one leg and a walrus mustache, stood in his front parlor with his back to a blistering fire. He had a shawl over one arm and a fan in one hand. He explained that he never knew when he might suffer a chill or a fever. In this atmosphere, Boyden met other trustees as well. One of them said to him, "It's a tossup whether the academy needs a new headmaster or an undertaker." They frankly did not know whether to hire him or close the school, but if he wanted the job he could have it.

In the village store, meanwhile, the town loafers had been assessing Boyden's style. In the recent past, they had seen plenty of new headmasters, and this one impressed the town about as little as the town had impressed him. He was, for one thing, five feet four inches tall. With his hair parted in the middle and with rimless spectacles, he looked forbidding but hardly forceful. Boys in that part of the state had been known to pick up schoolmasters and throw them out the window. It is still remembered that one of the men in the store that day said, "It won't be very long before they drive that young man out of here." Nothing is left of that scene—not even the store itself. Up the street, however, in the white frame house that once belonged to Ephraim Williams, lives the headmaster of Deerfield Academy. He has been the headmaster for sixty-four years.

[5]

During Boyden's first forty or fifty years in this position, he so concentrated on developing the character of the school that even after Deerfield had reached the highest peerage of American independent schools its students still slept in farmhouses and watched Saturday-night movies in a barn. Some New England prep schools were established in imitation of English public schools, but Deerfield is an indigenous institution. Boyden had been there twenty years before he added its boarding department, and since then he has tried not to allow Deerfield's gradual development from a local school into a national school to detach Deerfield from the advantages of its origin. The sons of rich people and of celebrated people compete to go there, and Deerfield accepts plenty of them, but it has a higher percentage of scholarship students than, for example, Andover, Exeter, Lawrenceville, Hotchkiss, Hill, Kent, Choate, Groton, St. Mark's, St. Paul's, and, for that matter, virtually every other major preparatory school. The average Deerfield scholarship is higher than the scholarships of nearly all other schools, and local boys still go to the academy for nothing. Boyden is now in a position to select his student body from among the top ten per cent of applicants, and his only competition in this respect comes from Andover and Exeter, but at first he had difficulty drawing students even from the town of Deerfield. With a borrowed horse and buggy, he went out into the fields of the surrounding Pocumtuck Valley and talked to young farm boys until he had persuaded them to go to school. He promised them days off at harvest, and in some cases he even paid for substitute farmhands. He continued to recruit students in this way for something over twenty years, and in successive bursts of generosity he gave up much of the personal money that he had meant to save for law school. Nonetheless, he went on reading law at night, having no intention, until he was in his late forties, of making education his permanent career. His school evolved naturally, gradually, and surprisingly. He had no plan and no theory, but he proved himself to be an educator by intuition. College professors and college presidents became aware of his work and sent their sons to him. Others did the same. By the late nineteen-thirties, it had become clear that he was one of the greatest headmasters in history, and for many years he has stood alone as, in all probability, the last man of his kind.

He is at the near end of a skein of magnanimous despots who—no matter whether they had actually founded the places or not—created enduring schools through their own individual energies, maintained them under their own absolute rule, and left them forever imprinted with their own personalities. At the other end is the prototype—Thomas Arnold, of Rugby. In the United States, Frank Boyden was for years the youngest in a group that included Endicott Peabody, of Groton; Father Sill, of Kent; Horace Taft, of Taft; Samuel

Drury, of St. Paul's; George C. St. John, of Choate; Alfred Stearns, of Andover; and Lewis Perry, of Exeter. The rest are gone now, and in some cases their successors are, too. Meanwhile, younger headmasters in remarkable numbers have developed under Boyden at Deerfield. At the moment, the heads of twenty-nine American prep schools are former Deerfield masters or students. Some headmasters similarly trained by Boyden have served their schools and have retired. But, in his valley in western Massachusetts, Frank Boyden, who is eighty-six, continues his work with no apparent letup, sharing his authority by the thimbleful with his faculty, travelling with his athletic teams, interviewing boys and parents who are interested in the school, conducting Sunday-night vesper services, writing as many as seventy letters a day, planning the details of new buildings, meeting with boys who are going home for the weekend and reminding them of their responsibilities to "the older travelling public," careering around his campus in an electric golf cart, and working from 7 A.M. to midnight every day. If he sees a bit of paper on the ground, he jumps out of his cart and picks it up. He is uncompromising about the appearance of his school, which has, in recent years, at last developed a physical plant that is appropriate to its reputation. The new academy buildings have been developed in consonance with the eighteenth-century houses of the town, a number of which the academy has, over the years, acquired. In all, thirty-three of the town's

[8]

old houses have been preserved. Two or three are used as dormitories. The front rooms of others have been turned into shrines of the American past and the back rooms into faculty apartments. As a municipal museum, Deerfield is of the nature and importance of Williamsburg, Virginia, with the difference that the buildings of Williamsburg are for the most part replicas and the houses of Deerfield are originals.

The Deerfield street is still the same quiet mile it was in 1902. Farmers still live along it. On the site of the old, sunless schoolhouse is the main building of the academy, and around and beyond it are nineteen other buildings— classrooms, dormitories, laboratories, gymnasiums, dining hall, hockey rink, infirmary, theatre, art gallery. The academy is on a kind of peninsular plateau that was formed when the Deerfield River, which flows through the valley, shifted its course in another age. On three sides, steep banks slope to a lower level, where there are perhaps seventy-five acres of athletic fields. Hills rise to the east and west, and there are long views of farmland and tobacco barns to the north and south. It would be difficult to imagine a more beautiful setting for a school or a more attractive school in the setting. What seems incredible, though, is that all of it—both the visible substance and the invisible essence of it—was developed by one man.

Ｐeople seeing the headmaster for the first time often find him different from what they expected. Those who stay in the Deerfield community for any length of time quickly become aware that they are living in a monarchy and that the small man in the golf cart is the king, but visitors who have heard of him and know what a great man he is seem to insist that he ought to be a tall, white-haired patriarch. People see him picking up papers and assume it is his job. Coming upon a group of women outside one of his old houses a few years ago, he took them in and led them through its ancient rooms. On the way out, one lady gave him a quarter. People walk right by him sometimes without seeing him. Someone once stopped, turned around, and said, "I'm sorry, Mr. Boyden. I didn't notice you."

"That's all right," he said. "No one ever does."

He loves such stories, perhaps in part because they help to fake out the faculty and the boys. How else, after all, could an inconspicuous man like that hold an entire community in the palm of his hand? When the stories come back to him, he lights up with pleasure. He has one way of judging everything: If it's good for the academy, it's good. He was once walking with an impressive-looking Deerfield faculty member when someone, a stranger, said, "Who was that?"

"That was the headmaster."

"Yes, but who was the little man with him?"

Boyden looked old when he was four, older when he was in college, and older still in the nineteen-twenties, but now he doesn't look particularly old at all. His hair is not white but slate-gray, and his demeanor, which hasn't changed in forty years, still suggests a small, grumpy Labrador. He sometimes dresses in gray trousers, a dark-blue jacket, and brown cordovan shoes—choices that are somewhat collegiate and could be taken as a mild sign of age, because for decades he wore dark-blue worsted suits and maroon ties almost exclusively, winter and summer, hanging on to each successive suit until it fell off him in threads. One of his jacket pockets today has a four-inch rip that has been bound with black thread. He doesn't care. He is an absolutely unself-conscious man. Let one scuff mark appear on a stair riser in his academy and he will quickly find a janitor and report it, but this kind of concern is entirely projected onto the school. He once got up on a cool July morning and put on an old leather coat covered with cracks and lined with sheepskin that was coming loose; he went off to New York in it and obliviously wore it all day in the sweltering city. After eighty-six years, his only impairment is bad hearing. "My ears are gone," he will say, and then he will walk into a roomful of people and pretend that there isn't a syllable he can't catch. He indulges himself in nothing. He will eat anything, and he usually doesn't notice the components of his meals, unless they happen to be root beer and animal crackers, which he occasionally eats for breakfast. He has been given honorary degrees by Harvard, Yale, Princeton, and seventeen other colleges and universities, but he apparently has not even a trace of a desire to be called Dr. Boyden, and no one calls him that except eraser salesmen and strangers whose sons are applying to the school.

"Never make a decision just to get something done," he says, and no one has ever accused him of being impulsive. His Director of Studies has said, "He has an infinite wisdom, which is as aggravating as hell. But anyone knowing him well who is faced with an important decision would go to him." This is, of course, most true of his students. They call him up in the summertime; they call him up from college; in later life, they call him up to ask if they should run for office. In conversation, he has the ability to give his undivided attention, and the perception to understand the implications of practically anything that is said to him. In this way, he has made several thousand people believe that he especially cares about them, which he does. He rarely loses his temper, but his capacity for absorbing criticism is not large. He is not proud in a narrow, personal sense; his pride is in his school and in his belief that he knows what is best for it. He is lost in the school, and there is nothing of him but the school. On vacation in Florida, he goes around in his blue worsted suit looking for people with money to help keep Deerfield going. He never goes near the water. He was once seen sitting in the lobby of the Breakers in Palm Beach reading a Deerfield yearbook. He is famous for his simplicity, which he cultivates. He is, in the highest sense, a simple man, and he has spent his life building a school according to elemental ideals, but only a complicated man could bring off what he has done, and, on the practical plane, he is full of paradox and politics. Senior members of his faculty, in various conversations, have described him as "a great humanitarian," "ruthless," "loyal," "feudal," "benevolent," "grateful," "humble," "impatient," "restless," "thoughtful," "thoughtless," "selfish," "selfless," "stubborn," "discerning," "intuitive," and "inscrutable"—never once disagreeing with one another. The headmaster's own view of himself, according to one of his two sons, is that he is "indestructible and infallible."

B OYDEN HAS THE GIFT of authority. He looks fragile, his voice is uncommanding, but people do what he says. Without this touch, he would have lost the school on the first day he worked there. Of the seven boys who were in the academy when he took over in that fall of 1902, at least four were regarded by the populace with fear, and for a couple of years it had been a habit of people of Deerfield to cross the street before passing the academy. Boyden's problem was complicated by one of the trustees, who was so eager to close the school that he had actually encouraged these boys to destroy the new headmaster as rapidly as they could. The boys were, on the average, a head taller and thirty pounds heavier than the headmaster. The first school day went by without a crisis. Then, as the students were getting ready to leave, Boyden said, "Now we're going to play football." Sports had not previously been a part of the program at the academy. Scrimmaging on the village common, the boys were amused at first, and interested in the novelty, but things suddenly deteriorated in a hail of four-letter words. With a sour look, the headmaster said, "Cut that out!" That was all he said, and—inexplicably—it was all he had to say.

A few days later, a boy asked him if he would like to go outside and have a catch with a baseball. The two of them went out onto the school lawn and stood about fifty feet apart. The boy wound up and threw a smokeball at him, apparently with intent to kill. Boyden caught the ball and fired it back as hard as he could throw it. A kind of match ensued, and the rest of the students collected to watch. The headmaster and the boy kept throwing the baseball at each other with everything they had. Finally, the boy quit. "Of course, I was wearing a glove and he wasn't," says the headmaster, who is a craftsman of the delayed, throwaway line.

He believed in athletics as, among other things, a way of controlling and blending his boys, and he required all of them to participate throughout the school year. This idea was an educational novelty in 1902. He arranged games with other schools, and because there were not enough boys in Deerfield Academy to fill out a football team or a baseball team, he jumped into the action himself. He was the first quarterback Deerfield ever had. He broke his nose and broke it again. Taking the ball in one game, he started around right end, but the other team's defensive halfback forced him toward the sideline, picked him up, and—this was years before the forward-motion rule—carried him all the way back to the Deerfield end zone and dumped him on the ground. He was a much better baseball player. Ignoring his height, he played first base. He was a good hitter, and Greenfield, Springfield, and Northampton newspapers of the time include items with headlines like "BOYDEN GOES 3 FOR 4 AS DEERFIELD ACADEMY BEATS ATHOL 2 TO 0." In sports, he captured and held his school, and it may be in sports that he developed the personal commitment that kept him there. His teammates were won over by him. Their earlier antagonism became support. He convinced them that the school would go under without their help, and they discovered that they wanted to keep it going as much as he did. In one game, at Arms Academy, he ran after a high pop foul, caught the ball two feet from a brick wall, crashed into it, and fell to the ground unconscious. The boys told him to go home and recover and not to worry—there would be no disciplinary problems at the school during his absence.

A teacher, Miss Minnie Hawks, was hired shortly after

the headmaster was, and she taught German and geometry while he taught algebra and physical geography. He used to take a rock into class with him, set it on his desk, and tell his students to write down everything they knew about the rock. But he was more interested in implications than he was in facts. His mind drifted quickly from science to behavior. "You're not youngsters anymore," he would say. "You're going to be the ones who run this town." He read a bit of the Bible to them every morning. Gradually, he acquired more teachers and spent less time in the classroom himself. He assembled a sound faculty and gave its members freedom to teach as they pleased. His own mark was made in moral education rather than in the academic disciplines. His first-hand relationship with his boys has always been extraordinary, and Deerfield students for sixty years have been characterized by the high degree of ethical sensitivity that he has been able to awaken in them. This is the area within which his greatness lies. From the start, he assumed responsibility not only for their academic development but also for their social lives, their recreation, and their religious obligations. He held dances, supplied dance cards, and, just to be sure that no one lacked interest, filled in the cards himself. After the dances, he got on the Greenfield-Northampton trolley car with his boys and girls and rode with them, making sure that each got off at the correct address. If he happened to be on the trolley's last run, he walked home—a distance of six

miles. He believed in wearing the boys out. They dug
ditches; they also made beehives, incubators, and wheelbarrows; and, with axes and crosscut saws, they cut
lumber for lockers for their athletic equipment. In his
first year, he set up a card table beside a radiator just
inside the front door of the school building. This was
his office, not because there was no room for a headmaster's office anywhere else but because he wanted
nothing to go on in the school without his being in the
middle of it. Years later, when the present main school
building was built, the headmaster had the architect design a wide place in the first-floor central hallway—the
spot with the heaviest traffic in the school—and that
was where his desk was put and where it still is. While
he dictates, telephones, or keeps his appointments, he
watches the boys passing between classes. He has a
remarkable eye for trouble. If the mood of the student
body at large is poor, he will sense it, and when one
boy is disturbed, he will see it in the boy's face, and he
will think of some minor matter they need to talk over,
so that he can find out what the difficulty is and try to
do something about it. He has maintained his familial
approach to education despite the spread of bureaucracy
into institutions and industries and despite the increased
size of his own school. In his early years, he found that
he could handle twenty-eight students as easily as fourteen, then fifty-six as easily as twenty-eight, and so on,
until, in the late nineteen-forties, he had something over

five hundred. The enrollment has remained at that level. "I can handle five hundred," he says. "Another hundred and I'd lose it."

Most schools have detailed lists of printed rules, and boys who violate them either are given penalties or are thrown out. A reasonable percentage of expulsions is a norm of prep-school life. Deerfield has no printed rules and no set penalties, and the headmaster has fired only five boys in sixty-four years. "For one foolish mistake, a boy should not have a stamp put on him that will be with him for the rest of his life," he says. "I could show you a list of rules from one school that is thirty pages long. There is no flexibility in a system like that. I'm willing to try a little longer than some of the other people do, provided there is nothing immoral. You can't have a family of three children without having some problems, so you have problems if you have five hundred. If you make a lot of rules, they never hit the fellow you made them for. Two hours after making a rule, you may want to change it. We have rules here, unwritten ones, but we make exceptions to them more than we enforce them. I always remember what Robert E. Lee said when he was president of Washington College, which is now Washington and Lee. He said, 'A boy is more important than any rule.' Ninety per cent of any group of boys will never get out of line. You must have about ninety per cent as a central core. Then the question is: How many of the others can you absorb?"

To say that Deerfield has no set rules is not to say that it is a place where a boy can experiment at will with his impulses. The academy has been described, perhaps fairly, as a gilded cage. The essential underlying difference between Deerfield and schools like Exeter and Andover is that Exeter and Andover make a conscious effort to teach independence and self-reliance by establishing a set of regulations to live by and then setting the boys free to stand or fall accordingly. Exeter and Andover boys can cut classes, within established margins, and they are provided with time they can call their own. Deerfield boys have several free hours each Sunday, but most of their time is programmed for them, and attendance is constantly taken. The headmaster's respect and admiration for Exeter and Andover are considerable, and he likes to quote a conversation he once had with an Andover headmaster, who said, "Maybe you're right. Maybe we're right. There is a need for both schools." Andover and Exeter, looking ahead to the college years, try to prepare their students for the freedom they will have, so that they can enjoy it and not suffer from it. Boyden believes that the timing of a boy's life requires more discipline in the secondary-school years than later, and that there is no point in going to college before you get there. "Boys need a sense of security," he says. "Discipline without persecution adds to that sense of security. People sometimes don't realize this, but boys like a control somewhere. We try to give them what you might call controlled freedom. We're the last bulwark of the old discipline. We're interested in new things, but I'm not going to throw away the fundamentals."

A new boy at Deerfield cannot have been there very long before the idea is impressed upon him that he is a part of something that won't work unless he does his share. The headmaster is able to create this kind of feeling in his boys to a greater degree than most parents are. All boys are given an equal footing from which to develop their own positions. There are no special responsibilities for scholarship boys, such as waiting on table. Everyone does that. In fact, the headmaster insists that scholarship boys not be told that they have scholarships, since that might injure the sense of equality he tries to build. His school, which grew so phenomenally out of almost nothing, has frequently been visited by curious educational theorists. One researcher spent a few days at the academy and finally said, "Well, there isn't any system here, but it works." Such people perplex Frank Boyden almost as much as he perplexes them. "People come here thinking we have some marvellous method," he says. "We just treat the boys as if we expect something of them, and we keep them busy. So many of our things simply exist. They're not theory. They're just living life. I expect most of our boys want to do things the way we want them done. We drive with a light rein, but we can pull it up just like that, if we need to. We just handle the cases as they come up."

His art as a disciplinarian often enables him to prevent things before they happen. He listens to the noise level in a group of boys, and watches the degree of restlessness; he can read these things as if they were a printed page. This is one reason he believes in meetings that involve the entire school. "You must have your boys together as a unit at least once a day, just as you have your family together once a day," he says. Evening Meeting is a Deerfield custom. The boys sit on a vast carpet in the anteroom of the school auditorium and listen to announcements, perhaps an anecdotal story from the headmaster, and reports of athletic contests and other activities. "Junior B Football beat the Holyoke High School Junior Varsity six to nothing this afternoon," says the coach of Junior B Football. "Charlie Hiller scored the touchdown with two minutes left in the game." In the applause that follows, this one low-echelon athlete gains something, and so does the school. On Sunday evenings, there is a vesper service, or Sunday Night Sing, as it is called, in which the boys sing one hymn after another, with a pause for a short talk by a visiting clergyman or educator. The lustre, or lack of it, in their voices is the headmaster's gauge of the climate of the student body for the week to come, and he accordingly chides them or exhorts them or amuses them or blasts them at Evening Meetings on succeeding days, often shaping his remarks around one of several precepts— "keep it on a high level," "be mobile," "finish up strong"

—which he uses so repeatedly and effectively that the words continue to ricochet through the minds of Deerfield graduates long after they leave the school. "He has the trick of the wrist with a whole community," one of his teachers has said.

All discipline ultimately becomes a private matter between each boy and the headmaster. Most of the boys feel guilty if they do something that offends his sensibilities. Unlike his great predecessor Arnold of Rugby, he does not believe that schoolboys are his natural enemies; on the contrary, he seems to convince them that although he is infallible, he badly needs their assistance. A local farmer who was in the class of 1919 says, "When you thought of doing something wrong, you would know that you would hurt him deeply, so you wouldn't do it. He had twenty-four-hour control." A 1928 alumnus says, "It didn't matter what you did as long as you told him the truth." And 1940: "Whatever it was, you didn't do it, because you might drop a little in his eyes." He will give a problem boy a second, third, fourth, fifth, and sixth chance, if necessary. The rest of the student body sometimes becomes cynical about the case, but the headmaster refuses to give up. "I would have kicked me out," says one alumnus who had a rather defiant senior year in the early nineteen-fifties. The headmaster had reason enough to expel him, and almost any other school would have dropped him without a thought, but Boyden graduated him, sent him to Princeton, and, today, does not even recall that the fellow was ever a cause of trouble. Boyden is incapable of bearing grudges. He wants to talk things out and forget them. He is sensitive to the potential effect of his forbearance, so he has sometimes taken the risk of calling the student body together and asking for its indulgence. A boy once drank the better part of a fifth of whiskey in a bus returning from another school, reeled in the aisle, fell on his face, and got sick. The headmaster called the school together and said that for the sake of discipline in the academy at large he would have to let the boy go unless they would guarantee him that no episode of the kind would happen again. The headmaster was beyond being thought of as weak, so he got away with it. People often wonder what on earth could make him actually drop a boy, and the five cases in which he has done so are therefore of particular interest. All have a common factor: the offender was unremorseful. One of them was guilty of nineteen different offenses, including arson. Nevertheless, if he had told the headmaster that he was wrong, he could have stayed in school.

A boy of considerable talent once told the headmaster that he could write his English papers only between midnight and dawn. His muse, the boy claimed, refused to appear at any other time of day. The difficulty was that after the boy's inspiration ran out he invariably fell asleep and missed his morning classes. Like all geniuses, this boy was likely to attract imitators. The headmaster addressed the student body. "Are you willing to let Mac Farrell stay up all night writing his English papers?" he said. "Mac Farrell alone?" The boys agreed.

The headmaster has often put himself in an uncomfortable corner for a boy who is different. He once had two students—artistic cousins of Mac Farrell—who liked to paint and particularly liked to go out at night and do nocturnes. They did the cemetery by moonlight and the old houses in the edge of the glow of street lamps. The headmaster knew that this was going on, but he overlooked it. His own favorites have always been responsible, uncomplicated, outstanding athletes, and he cares even less about art than he knows about it, but, in his way, he was just the right headmaster for these two boys. "With a person as unDeerfield as myself," remembers one of them, who is now Curator of Graphic Arts at Princeton University, "he was sympathetic and understanding. He was patient and—what can I say?— incredibly wise in the way that he handled me."

Certain boys at Deerfield in earlier years would commit long series of petty crimes and believe that all had gone undetected. Then, finally, the headmaster would stop such a boy, pull out a small notebook, and read off to him everything he had done wrong since the first day of school. For years, the headmaster roved the campus late at night, like a watchman. Until the late nineteen-thirties, he made rounds to every room in every dormitory during study hours every night. Since then, he has made spot visits. He never gives a boy bad news at night. He never threatens. He uses shame privately. He more often trades favors than gives them. If a boy asks something of him, he asks something in return. There is no student government, nor are there faculty committees, helping to run Deerfield. The headmaster holds himself distant from that sort of thing. Senior-class presidents are elected on the eve of Commencement. Students who are in the school now say they would not want student government anyway, because they feel that it is a mockery elsewhere.

BOYDEN'S PRINCIPLE of athletics for all has remained one of the main elements of the school's program, and Deerfield is unmatched in this respect today.
Where once he did not have enough boys for even one
team, he now has teams for all five hundred. When a
boy at Deerfield chooses a sport, he automatically makes
a team that has a full schedule of games with other
schools. For example, Deerfield usually has at least eight
basketball teams, each with game uniforms, away games,
and all the other incidentals of the sport on the varsity
level. This is true in soccer, baseball, football, tennis,

lacrosse, hockey, squash, swimming, skiing, track, and cross-country as well. With few exceptions, every boy at Deerfield is required to take part in three sports a year. There is no set number of teams in any sport. According to the boys' choices, there may be a few more football teams one year and a few more soccer teams the next. Deerfield has sent on a share of athletic stars—football players such as Mutt Ray to Dartmouth and Archie Roberts to Columbia, for instance—but Deerfield is not really an atmosphere in which a great athlete is likely to develop. The headmaster's belief in sport is exceeded by his belief that everything has its place and time. Deerfield athletes are given no time for extra practice, nor are they permitted to practice any sport out of season. In the fall and the spring, the basketball courts are locked, and baskets are actually removed from the backboards.

In the early days, having the headmaster as a player produced some disadvantages for Deerfield teams. Once, in a pick-off situation in baseball, when he caught the throw from the pitcher and put his glove down, the opposing player slid safely under him. "Out," said the umpire. Any other baseball player would have congratulated himself on his luck, but the headmaster had to tell the umpire that the fellow had in fact been safe. From the start, he had been preaching sportsmanship to his boys. People who remember those days say that he was the first person in that part of the country to stress courtesy in athletics. "We may wish they were interested in other things," he said at the time, "but we must meet existing conditions, and since they will have athletic sports anyway, let us control them and make them a moral force." No matter how able a Deerfield player was or how close a game had become, if he showed anger he was benched. If a basketball player said anything the least bit antagonistic to the man he was guarding—even something as mild as "Go ahead and shoot"—a substitute would go into the game. Athletics was one of the ways in which Deerfield became known, and from the beginning the headmaster wanted his teams to be smartly dressed and thoroughly equipped. In the early years, he often spent at least a third of his salary on athletic equipment, and when a woman of the town offered a contribution to the school, he asked if he might use it for baseball uniforms. "Something has lifted the spirit of this community," she said to him. "Go and buy the best uniforms you can find, but don't tell anyone I gave the money for it."

The headmaster played on Deerfield teams until he was about thirty-five, and he was head coach of football, basketball, and baseball until he was nearly eighty. "I can't go to a funeral anywhere from Athol to Northampton without an elderly man's coming up and reminding me of a baseball game we once played against one another," he says. His sense of football has always been vague but imaginative. His blocking assignments were not precise. During his years as player-coach, he put straps on the belts of his linemen so that the backs—himself included—could hang on and be pulled forward for short gains. In baseball, he followed a simple strategy. "If you can put your glove on a fast ball, there is no reason you can't put your bat on it," he has said for sixty-four years. "Anyone can learn to bunt." Deerfield teams use the squeeze play as if there were no alternative in the sport. He continued to hit fungoes to his baseball teams until he was seventy-five years old. It was a high point of any Deerfield baseball day to watch him hit precise grounders to his scrambling infield. Toward the end of his coaching years, the headmaster found that he could not hit the ball with quite as much snap as he liked to give it. He complained that the ground was getting softer. His main talent as a coach was that he always seemed to know what a boy could do and then expected no more of him. He knew, somehow, when a pitcher was almost through. If his assistant coaches happened to prevail on him to leave a pitcher in a game, disaster usually followed. What he did not know about football he made up through his knowledge of boys, and he could win a game with the right remark. He once did so—in the early nineteen-twenties—by taking his quarterback aside and saying to him, "You're just like a race horse. Sometimes you're too tense to do your job. Take it easy. You'll run faster."

Visitors today sometimes think that the headmaster

is a little theatrical when he walks up and down the sidelines—eighty-six years old, and wearing a player's duffel coat that almost reaches the ground—and acts as if he were on the verge of jumping into the game. Something they may not be able to imagine is what it must mean to him to remember the games against small local schools when he himself was in the backfield and there were fifteen or twenty boys in the academy, and now, more than sixty years later, to be watching his team make one touchdown after another until the final score is Deerfield 28, Exeter 0. As a semi-retired coach, the headmaster still gives the same pre-game talks he has always given. In a way that is desperate, unyielding, and total, he wants to win, but he wants to win with grace. "The consequence of poor sportsmanship is that you lose, somewhere along the line," he says. "Remember, it's better to lose in a sportsmanlike way than to win and gloat over it." And he goes along in that vein for a while, until he has satisfied the requirements of his conscience. Then he says, "Now, boys, let's not let up on them for a minute. Let's win this one, if possible, by forty points."

THE HEADMASTER has never thought of Deerfield wholly, or even largely, as a preparatory school. He thinks that the education a secondary school offers has to be considered in its own right and in all its aspects, and that the school is not merely a conduit to college. "Things can be done at our level which they can't do in college," he says. "Dean Henry Pennypacker at Harvard always used to say, 'After a man is thirty, he is going to settle most of his social and moral problems in terms of his training in secondary school.' My philosophy—I can't express it, really: I believe in boys. I believe in keeping them busy, and in the highest standards of scholarship. I believe in a very normal life. It generally seeps in. I try to do the simple things that a well-organized home does for its boys." When he expresses these ideas, and uses a phrase such as "normal life," he is drawing, in the main, on his own boyhood, in Foxboro, Massachusetts. "Basically, it is an acceptance of the code of that era," he says. "The home was dominant, you see."

Foxboro, about halfway between Boston and Providence, was a town of about twenty-five hundred people when Boyden was a boy. It contributed importantly to the straw-hat industry, and it had an iron foundry, which had been established to cast cannon for the Continental Army in the American Revolution and had more recently supplied New York City with its red fire-alarm boxes. Boyden's family owned the foundry. His father and mother, who had both been schoolteachers in their early years, had settled into the foundry business before he was born. Like everyone else in the town, they had a few cows and horses, chickens, and a pig. They had a hundred and fifty acres of land and raised their own vegetables. "In those days, people raised everything they ate," the headmaster says. "I can't understand it when I see these farmers today, with so much land, buying their own vegetables." He was born in 1879 in the family's large white frame farmhouse, a building that is still an attractive place. In the subtle gradations of Foxboro society, there were people in the town center who pre-ferred not to mix with the people in the section known as South Foxboro. "We were halfway to the center," the headmaster remembers, and this intermediate posi-tion has served him well.

His family had been in Massachusetts since 1634, when an indentured servant named Thomas Boyden arrived from England and went to work in Salem. Thomas Boy-den prospered sufficiently to pay off his debt, become a freeman, and contribute one bushel of wheat to the establishment of "the new brick college"—Harvard. Seth Boyden, a great-uncle of the headmaster, was one of those people whom the term "Yankee ingenuity" was coined to describe. He devised the first patent leather and produced the first daguerreotype in the United States, and he developed malleable iron. The headmaster in-herited none of this. He hates machines, and, in fact, is suspicious of anything inanimate that has moving parts. His Grandfather Cary—his mother's father—owned the iron foundry and was, in many ways, an earlier version of the headmaster. He was known as the Little Man, he still had iron-gray hair when he was in his seventies, and his employees would say, "If you hunt for him, you will never find him, but stand still in one place and within five minutes the Little Man will come around." All this precisely describes the headmaster, and, as a mat-ter of fact, he is known in Deerfield as the Little Man.

His Grandfather Cary served in the Massachusetts Senate and Assembly, and so did the headmaster's father, Benjamin Franklin Boyden, a man who has been remembered as a bit of a Micawber with a gift for words. The headmaster's mother was more simply designed. "She was quiet, and a very good Sunday-school teacher," he says. "She was a gracious and devout religious person. A great deal of our life centered on the Congregational church. I used to go to three services on Sunday. The only reason I didn't go to four is that there wasn't a fourth one, I'm sure of that." Deerfield boys go to two services on Sunday. The first is beyond the headmaster's control, because it is in the hands of one clergyman or another in the area; the second, the Sunday Night Sing, is made palatable by his selection of rousing and familiar hymns —one verse, two at the most. He says that when he was young he belonged to "a tough Sunday-school class." A photograph of him in his Sunday-school clothes at that time does not make him look very tough, but there is a kind of reinforced gravity in his eyes which suggests that if this little boy were to clap his hands, everyone within earshot would fall silent. Around his neck is something that resembles a lace doily, and there are pouches under his eyes. He was the third of four children. He read a lot as a little boy, played backgammon every night with an aunt, and went to a one-room school that was named for his maternal grandfather. In icy weather,

which came often, he skated to school, passing a cran-
berry bog and stands of scrub oak and pine, and crossing
ponds to which his family owned flowage rights.

Throughout his years in Deerfield, he has visited Foxboro with great frequency. He reads the Foxboro paper
every week, and says, "I'd be lost without it." The town
is still his home, though none of his family is there. He
points into a forest of high white pines in Foxboro and
says, "That was our mowing lot. In a dry summer, you
couldn't get anything out of it—not even hay. We used
to play baseball there." The Foxboro library, a small
nineteenth-century building that looks like a gingerbread
house, is called the Boyden Library, as it was when the
headmaster was a boy. Around the town common is an
exceptionally graceful iron fence, which his Grandfather
Cary designed and wrought in his foundry. Driving
through a section of woodland, the headmaster gestures
toward a dry stream bed in a broad hollow filled with
tall deciduous trees. "The foundry was right in there,"
he says. "It was quite sizable. The men were fine mold-
ers. Seventy people worked there." He confides that
many of them were heavy drinkers, and he adds that
because of this he has always been able to identify a
problem drinker at sight. How? "There is something in
the face of a man from the lips up."

Boyden went to Foxboro High School and was graduated with the class of 1896. He was sixteen years old.
"That's too young," he says. "I had no competition in

high school, and when I finished I had no interest in education." His school today takes part in advanced-placement programs, but only because the universality of the idea has forced the headmaster to go along with it. He clearly feels that an individual's development is in danger of being hurt if it is accelerated. On the other hand, if there had been an advanced-placement program at Foxboro High School in the eighteen-nineties he might not have lost interest in education. He had no desire to go to college. Instead, he went to work in a grocery store. He got to be such an expert grocer that it irritated him when new employees came into the store and got the handle of the lard tub greasy. "There was a way to manage the handle without getting it greasy," he says, "but it took experience." He also worked for his father, driving a horse and buggy between the train station and the foundry five trips a day. Eventually, all this palled, and his intellectual curiosity came back to life. He decided to take examinations for admission to Amherst College, which meant that he had to learn Latin and Greek within nine months and also recondition his English, mathematics, and history. "I got my power of concentration then," he says. "I had to."

After Boyden's class—1902—had been at Amherst for one term, more than a sixth of its members were flunked out. "I was so green, so small, and so scared I'd be sent home that I just stayed in my room and worked and worked and worked," the headmaster remembers. Like all the other freshmen, he was interviewed by Amherst's eleven fraternities. The next step in the screening process was a second interview by fraternities that were interested. Boyden was invited to no second interviews at all. "I was ruled off as a cipher," he says. "And it was true. It was a fair judgment. I just boned away everlastingly." His classmates began to call him Plugger Bill. None of those who are still alive can give a satisfactory explanation why they chose Bill. One of them says, "We called him that because it was euphonious." Whatever the reason, he has always been called Bill by his Amherst friends. "I never liked the Plugger part," the headmaster says now. "I like the name Bill very much. I can't stand Frank." His classmates came to know him in later years much better than they had known him at Amherst, and some of them, as trustees of Deerfield Academy, more than once helped to keep the school out of bankruptcy. Two of them are still living, and their recollections of Boyden at Amherst are valuable, if not wholly flattering. "Plugger Bill Boyden expresses it," says Robert J. Cleeland, the retired president of a candy company in Springfield. "He didn't make any impression on me at all. He was a midnight-oil burner. Our paths didn't cross. I was involved in athletics. He was Plugger Bill Boyden. There's something about that fellow. You stand him up in a line of ten people and try to pick the successful man, you'd pick him tenth. He was unknown in the class, and he is the biggest man the class produced. Perhaps you can tell the fertility of a seed by looking at it, but I don't think you can." Robert W. Maynard, the chairman of R. H. Stearns Company, the Boston department store, describes 1902 as "a tail-ender class," and says, "No one ever thought we would amount to anything. The first time I saw Bill was at the freshman-sophomore baseball game on Blake Field. He was out for the team, this little bit of a cub. He didn't make it. He was good at his studies, he liked athletics, he worked hard. Phi Kappa Psi finally took him in. It was a new fraternity then. A lot of waifs and strays were taken in there."

While Boyden was learning what it was like to be thought of as a stray, he was also learning what it was like to be relatively poor. A fire destroyed the foundry in Foxboro, which was uninsured. During his sophomore year in college, he had so little money that he once felt guilty about the expense when he bought an ice-cream cone. As interested as he was in athletics, he never made a team, because he was too small. (His own version is that he was not good enough.) He managed the tennis team. He was an accomplished debater, and he was impressed by the singing at Amherst; two of the most luminous features of Deerfield Academy are its debating teams and its superb glee clubs. Charles Edward Garman, professor of mental and moral philosophy, was one of the few people at Amherst who apparently saw Boyden's potentialities. Garman told him that he would become a fine lawyer. The headmaster describes Garman as "one of the great teachers in America," and says that Garman turned down college deanships and presidencies because he preferred to stay at Amherst and help send people like Dwight Morrow into the world. On the many occasions when Boyden himself could have accepted headmasterships at wealthy and established schools, his affectionate memories of Garman helped to keep him at Deerfield. A note in the 1902 Amherst senior classbook said, "Magill won over Boyden by one vote as the man whom the college has benefited the most."

THERE WERE ONCE academies in almost all the towns of New England, and most of them are now, if anything, just outlines in the lawns of other buildings. It is often said that Frank Boyden would have created a major school from any one of these relics wherever he happened to go, and that it was an accident fortunate for Deerfield that he happened to go there. Some families of Deerfield think otherwise, however, and there is much in what they have to say. The sum of it is that he was lucky to come upon such a town.

Deerfield, in the seventeenth century, was the principal settlement on the Massachusetts frontier. Its first minister was a Mather. Its first baby had the annunciatory name of Mehuman Hinsdell. Its first Indian raid wiped out the town. Some people escaped, and a few of them returned. Then, during Queen Anne's War, a French general in Canada dispassionately planned the murder of the town, augmented his forces with two Indian tribes, and made the long march south in winter. Deerfield lived in ignorance of this condemnation until the night of February 29, 1704, when the Indians rushed in over the snow, pausing, rushing, pausing, rushing—absurdly, perhaps successfully, trying to disguise their sounds as gusts of wind. On drifted snow, they vaulted the palisades and they chopped their way into houses with tomahawks, shrieking even more loudly than the people they were shooting and axing to pieces. The French watched with no apparent emotion. Forty-eight people were buried in a common grave in a cemetery that is now within the grounds of the academy. On the nearby grave of Mehuman Hinsdell, the inscription says that he was "twice captivated by the Indian savages." A raid of reprisal in Nova Scotia became the background for Longfellow's "Evangeline." In Deerfield today, two of the old houses pre-date the Deerfield Massacre, as it is called, but most of the others were built during the quiet and prosperous period that followed, between Queen Anne's War and the American Revolution. Deerfield declared its independence in *June* of

1776. Colonel Benedict Arnold bought food there for the Continental Army. The academy was established in 1797, and for about fifty years it attracted students not only from the town of Deerfield but also from other towns and states. Eventually, it diminished into a small, entirely local school.

In the nineteenth century, Deerfield first became something of a tourist attraction. John Quincy Adams said that the village and the valley were "not excelled by anything I have ever seen, not excepting the Bay of Naples." It apparently attracted all kinds, for John L. Sullivan stayed there and so did Francis Parkman and Ralph Waldo Emerson. The town became an art colony of some importance. By the time the headmaster arrived, in 1902, there was a dedicated group of citizens who were already determined that Deerfield's old houses should be preserved. Such people would not have been found in just any New England town. One of them, George Sheldon, an old man with a tapering white beard at least a foot and a half long, had written a two-volume history of the town, three hundred and fifty thousand words long and composed with a high degree of literary skill. When people were in church or out of town, he went into their attics and removed artifacts of Colonial days in the interests of posterity. His wife, Jennie Arms Sheldon, the woman who gave the headmaster the money for baseball uniforms, had been educated at M.I.T. and was one of the first females ever enrolled there. Deerfield was, in a sense, under the control of cultivated women, most of whom were spinsters —Miss Whiting, Miss Coleman, Miss Baker, Miss Miller. They made baskets, held art shows, conducted a literary salon, and, collectively, were the single most potent political force in the community. To some of these people, the young headmaster soon appeared to be "an upstart trying to run the town." He was not, after all, Old Deerfield. Boyden, in 1902, had walked into a town that would shape him as much as he would shape it.

IT HELPED THE HEADMASTER that he married a Deerfield girl. Helen Childs' father was a dairy farmer and also a highway contractor and builder of wooden bridges. In 1896, when she was thirteen, her father arranged for her to go to Greenfield High School, five miles up the road, because she wanted to try for Smith College and he felt, reasonably, that Deerfield Academy was inadequate for someone with such an ambition. She was graduated from Smith in the class of 1904, and after teaching briefly in a school in Connecticut she accepted an offer from Frank Boyden, the new headmaster, to teach science and mathematics at the academy. They were married in 1907.

With interruptions for the birth of their children—two sons and a daughter—she has been on the Deerfield faculty for sixty-one years. Her reputation as a teacher of chemistry grew quickly, and it has stood for decades among the highest in secondary education. She is everything a headmaster's wife could possibly be—gentle, understanding, forgiving, irreverent about her husband; but beyond this, she is the brightest person on the faculty and the busiest employee of the school. She is eighty-two now. She teaches five hours a day, meeting more classes than any other Deerfield teacher. "She is much more important than I am," the headmaster says. "She has a wonderful sense of humor and deep affection for the boys. She has more influence on the boys than I have. She makes them want to do the work. Her judgment is excellent. It is interesting that a combination such as the two of us could get together. I don't know that I've ever known her, really. She could have been the head of any school." Mrs. Boyden reads a book or two a week and keeps up thoroughly with what is going on in the world—much more so than the headmaster does. He is totally immersed in the school and travels only for school purposes. Her interests have no limit. When she was planning to go up the Nile a couple of years ago, she read histories of Egypt for a full year in advance. She also reads the books that people are talking about, and when it is her turn to do the talking she invariably has something original to say. Her husband seems at base to be an emotional man; she is more logical. "She is very feminine," the headmaster says, "and she wouldn't like it if I said this, but she has a man's mind."

In class, she is a drillmaster, with the important qualification that she uses rote as a device rather than an end in itself. She may be discussing, say, isotopes. "Wait just a minute, young man," she says. "What about the atomic structure of isotopes? . . . Right. Where do they differ? . . . In the nucleus." Her gray-white hair is swept high on her head. She often wears a pearl choker, a silver bracelet, a gold watch, a silver pin. Her glasses are tortoise shell across the top; the bottom rims are clear. She can't really see anyone in the room, because she is nearsighted to the point of partial blindness. She knows who her students are by the seats she has assigned to them. She may not be able to see them clearly, but she knows when something is not right. Once, she broke off in the middle of a sentence and said, "George Gallup, do you have a shirt on?" There was young George Gallup in the third row with his sports-jacket collar turned up around his neck and an embarrassed explanation about having failed to send his shirts to the laundry. Because of her handicap, her memory has developed phenomenally. An alumnus visits her classroom—an event so frequent that the room almost never seems to be without one—and she says to him when he enters, "Why don't you sit where you used to sit, in the second seat from the windows in the next-to-last row?" He may have been graduated from Deerfield seventeen years earlier, but she is right. On the blackboard, she has written, "The sins we commit two by two, we pay for one by one." The next day, she has written, "There are few concepts so difficult that they do not yield to the repeated attack of the ordinary mind." She has moved on to a discussion of the overthrow of the phlogiston theory. "I hope none of you smoke," she puts in. "As I get old, I'm getting awfully arbitrary." She plays games with the boys, giving them gradeless quizzes, asking one short question after another, drawing them out as if they were around a dinner table. "Victor," she said to one, years ago, "when will you stop trying to remember and start trying to think?" Victor Butterfield is the president of Wesleyan University, and that is his most highly valued story about his own education. At the end of the hour, the buzzer sounds, and she goes right on talking. Minutes pass, and another class collects in the doorway, but she is still talking. Her classes end this way more often than not.

Mrs. Boyden gets up every morning at six and works in her greenhouse until breakfast. She studies in her office during free periods in the school day. The normal class day consists of six periods, ends at 2 P.M., and is followed by a conference period for supplementary discussion with students who need it. Each faculty member holds one conference period a week, except Mrs. Boyden, who holds one every day. She also spends Saturday mornings with students who need special help, and many afternoons and evenings as well. During College Board tests, she walks the school-building corridors with anxiety and is outside the door when her students emerge, to ask them how they did. She often has luncheon guests, and a couple of nights a week there are guests for dinner. Every evening, she pours after-dinner coffee in her living room for about fifty people. She goes to Sunday Night Sing, in part because she is expected to. She has been the official scorer of Deerfield baseball games since the First World War. She goes to all the home football and basketball games and to most of the away games as well. She arrives at the Deerfield pool a full hour before swimming meets and sits there knitting in the concrete grandstand, because she refuses the privilege of having a seat saved for her and does not want to precipitate a situation in which boys would feel obliged to move. She was feeling both weak and exhausted one day recently when she was supposed to go off in the evening to a glee-club concert in Hartford. "At your age, you wouldn't need to go," she said to a younger teacher. "At my age, I *have* to go."

She can sketch the headmaster in fine lines. "He had a very unhumorous background," she says. "I am a Unitarian, and he is a Congregationalist. I think his family would have preferred that he marry a Buddhist." Their wedding was a large one, with many bridesmaids and four hundred guests, and the reception was held in the academy. She says that the headmaster disappeared during the reception and was found delivering a talk to a group of boys on how they should behave going home in the trolley. When her daughter was born—in their home on the campus—and she was just emerging from the effects of ether and did not know quite where she was, the headmaster burst into the room and said, "Helen, what are we going to do about the trustees? They're being so difficult." The Boydens' daughter, Elizabeth, now teaches history at Stoneleigh-Prospect Hill, a girls' school near Deerfield. Their younger son, Ted, is director of the Center for Business and Economic Education at Georgia State College. And their older son, John, is director of admissions at Deerfield.

Mrs. Boyden was ready to return to teaching after the birth of her third child, but the headmaster was not certain that he approved. A few months later, a chemistry teacher quit. There were no other prospects in sight. The headmaster turned to his wife. She fenced with him and made him ask her twice, because she wanted so desperately to have the job. He said, "All right, you can do it for a year. But I don't think a woman should work for her husband. I want you to understand that if you ever have any disciplinary trouble with a boy, I will be on the side of the boy." For years and years, even when she had become one of the most brilliant teachers in her field, she feared that she might lose her job.

Like many people at Deerfield, Mrs. Boyden calls her husband the Head Man. More than anyone else, of course, she sees him plying and politicking and telling white lies in order to avoid collisions in the general flow of the school. She smiles at the remark of Victor Butterfield, who says, "There has to be a strategy as well as an ideal. Only petty people would fail to understand this." Her husband is a master politician. Sometimes, when he is about to put a spur into students or faculty, he will say, "Now, the board of trustees feels . . ." And the board of trustees, of course, is feeling nothing at all. Often, when he wants to offer constructive criticism to a young teacher, he spares both himself and the younger man by introducing the subject in this way: "Some of the senior faculty members are a little disturbed by this, and they have talked to me." In reference to these devices, Mrs. Boyden says, "At times, the truth simply is not in that man."

The headmaster has never had a drink or a smoke in his life. She will have sherry before lunch. "He makes his boys be neat," she says, "but around here he throws everything on the floor. I spend half my time looking for the things he loses. He'll keep his anger in the house, and then go out and be sweet with the faculty and the boys. His father was like that. Just and gracious to other people, but how he yips at his family! He is a progressive-minded person, but he will cling to the old with tenacity. He is the least scientific person in the world. He has the craziest ideas. But what is it that makes a person have such strength? Why do I always do what he tells me to do? He wasn't interested in education when he was sixteen, and he isn't now. In a larger way, though, he is a man who believes that education equals public welfare. That's not a small thing to be. Anyone can be interested in the Latin derivations of words."

Yale once gave the headmaster an honorary degree for "research work in the hearts and minds of boys." Smith gave Mrs. Boyden one with a citation that read, "To Helen C. Boyden, who, with some small help from her husband, built a great school." When they are together, she makes light of him and he reacts in kind. She is the quicker of the two. He is funnier.

"You can't carry a grudge," she said to him recently, over afternoon tea. "You don't have a mean streak in you. You have plenty of other failings."

"Yes, don't forget to add that," he said.

He acknowledged her seniority in the community. "When I came here, she had been here for two hundred and fifty years," he said.

"You can't get around it," she said to him. "You're an interloper."

"Yes," he said. "But I came by choice."

Asked what era they thought had been the best at Deerfield, they both answered at once.

"1906," said the headmaster.

"1966," said his wife.

THE HEADMASTER first became known among educators for his achievements with unlikely material. In the kind of language that modern academicians sometimes use, there was a high salvage factor in his work. He seemed to know when there was something in a boy when on the surface there appeared to be nothing. He could assess this potentiality in a way that no test could, and he had the talent to help the boy reach it. In the nineteen-twenties, Deerfield regularly had a number of students who, for disciplinary or academic reasons, had been kicked out of places like Andover, Exeter, and Taft.

After a year or two at Deerfield, a considerable number of these boys out-performed their former Exeter, Andover, or Taft classmates in college. This was not only gratifying to Boyden but also both pleasing and relieving to other headmasters, who suddenly found that with clear consciences they could fire almost any boy, since Frank Boyden could be counted on to turn the lout into an interested scholar and a useful citizen.

Boyden had developed this special skill partly as a result of his early work with the farm boys of the valley, whose education, in most cases, would have lapsed without his persistence. In one of these, a boy in the Deerfield class of 1911, the headmaster found a kind of objectification of his idea of Deerfield. Being an intuitive and untheoretical man, he has never tried to express in any definitive way the kind of goal he has tried to reach. Instead, he tells the story of Tom Ashley. As a thirteen-year-old boy, Ashley, one gathers, was uncommunicative to the verge of moroseness. He disclosed no intellectual curiosity. He had been born to farming, he loved the open, and he kept a notebook of the achievements he considered important enough to record. "Rifle, game shot," begins one entry, covering a brief segment of 1907. "Blue jays—1, red squirrels—3, muskrats—6, skunks—15, cats—3, mud turtles—1, snakes—1, rats—3, pigs—1, doves—8." On March 23rd of that year, the boy noted that he "went swimming first time, had to wade through snowdrift to get in the water." A note soon thereafter says, "Began haying July 15, 1907. 1. Great Pasture. 2. Wright's Yard. 3. The Island. 4. The Neck. 5. Pine Hill. 6. Pug's Hole. 7. Black Snake Piece. 8. Great Bottom. 9. Little Plain. Ended haying August 5."

In the following month, the boy so intractably refused to enter the academy that his father seemed ready to write him off as a clod, and the headmaster made no apparent effort to influence him. There happened, however, to be a great stack of schoolbooks that needed moving, and would Tom please lend a hand before going off to shoot another pig, or whatever he was going to do? Ashley helped, without speaking. The academy was so short of football players, the headmaster told him, that although he was not actually in the school, he could play with the other boys that afternoon if he wanted to; meanwhile, the headmaster would be grateful if he would hold the door open for some visitors who happened to be coming up the walk. There was something romantic in Ashley, because he went to football practice that afternoon wearing a skate strap so that he could repair a leg fracture, if necessary, without leaving the field. Within a short time, he was enrolled in the academy. He was a well-proportioned fellow, and he proved to be an excellent athlete, replacing the headmaster in the backfield of the football team and becoming a teammate of the headmaster in baseball. For four years, he seldom said anything in class or to the girls, but, at the headmaster's request, he delivered a speech at the 1911 Commencement exercises, and it was moving, if for no other reason than that he was actually talking.

Ashley went on to Amherst and began a steady correspondence with the headmaster, which was full of hopes, worries, reports of his grades, football plays for use at Deerfield, requests for advice, and minor apologies such as "I hate to bother you with such small matters, but I would like to know how you see it before approaching my father." Ashley was the captain of the Amherst basketball team and a star in football and baseball. He majored in history and decided to become a teacher.

His story, in its essential elements, has been repeated at Deerfield a thousand times, and it has served as a kind of standard. In memory, Ashley has become more of an ideal than an actual person, but fifty years ago he was probably the closest friend the headmaster had ever had. He joined the Deerfield faculty in 1916. He cared enormously about the school, and he had much bigger ideas for it than had ever crossed the headmaster's mind; he envisioned it as a large national academy, drawing students from numerous states. He drafted a prospectus of the expanded academy and sketched a map of future halls and dormitories. He urged the headmaster to start moving in that direction by reviving the boarding department, which had been inactive for seventy years. There were a few boarders in the school at the time— boys whose fathers had heard of the headmaster's early achievements and had arranged for their sons to live with families in the town. Ashley suggested that thirty-five students from outside Deerfield might be a good number to expand to right away. "We'll never have thirty-five boarders here," the headmaster said, with a swampy look —not because he did not want them but because he could not imagine so many boarders being there. Ashley died in a wheat field near Château-Thierry. He was trying to get a captured German machine gun to work, so that he could turn it against another German machine gun, which killed him. John Lejeune, the commandant of the United States Marine Corps, in whose office Ashley had first volunteered for service, later sent a personal check to the headmaster and asked that some sort of tablet be put up at Deerfield in memory of Lieutenant Ashley. The headmaster used the money to help build a dormitory for boys from other towns and states.

Soon after the war, John Winant, who was later to become Governor of New Hampshire and United States Ambassador to the Court of St. James's, made a visit to Deerfield, spent a day with the headmaster, and admitted to him during the afternoon that he had come as a representative of the Brearley School, in New York, whose trustees had asked him to see if the headmaster of Deerfield would like to become the headmaster of Brearley. "However, I am not going to make the offer," Winant said. "What you are doing here is obviously too important, and this is where you should stay." Winant, who later sent his sons to Deerfield, did not say how much Brearley was offering, and the headmaster was too polite to ask. He had been sincerely tempted by other offers, some of which would have doubled his salary, and, of course, there was always the law, to which his commitment was regularly postponed on a June-to-June basis. "When I had been here seven years, I didn't see many possibilities, and I began to think more and more about the law," he says, remembering one black period. "I was pretty much discouraged." On another of these occasions, he was about to accept a different job and leave Deerfield, but he opened the Bible, and, he says, the first passage his eye fell on was Jeremiah 42:10: "If ye will still abide in this land, then will I build you, and not pull you down, and I will plant you, and not pluck you up: for I repent me of the evil that I have done unto you." He decided to stay. He tells that story often. His wife says that she believes it is true but that he has probably condensed it by leaving out the number of times he opened the Bible before he found a passage that would satisfy him. On still another occasion when he was about to quit, a priest from South Deerfield learned about it and told him, "You can't. You are the only man in the town of Deerfield who can go into every home in the valley. Now get back to work."

By 1923, there were one hundred and forty students in the academy. Eighty were boarding students. The son of the president of Cornell was there, and the son of the president of what is now the University of Massachusetts, and so were grandsons of the presidents of Amherst, Smith, and Vassar, and sons of deans or professors at—among other places—the University of California, Mount Holyoke, Williams, Harvard, the College of the City of New York, and George Washington University. This endorsement of his work was gratifying to the headmaster, but for the moment he was too deeply concerned to enjoy it, because a section of the new Massachusetts constitution appeared to signal the closing of the school. The law said that public funds could not be used for the support of a private school. Deerfield Academy, which was now partly a private school and partly a public school, was receiving twenty thousand dollars a year from the town of Deerfield and was going to founder without it. If the academy were to close its boarding department and continue as solely a public high school, not only would much of the headmaster's work be undone but a new and heavy concentration of population in South Deerfield, six miles away, would force the school to be relocated there, removing it from the original settlement, of which it was by now an integral part. Moreover, a legal battle broke out that filled up column upon column of Massachusetts newsprint. The technical area of contention was framed in the terms of a bequest that had been made to the town in 1878 by a woman whose will directed that the income from the bequest be used to support the school. The question was: Could the academy—in order to become a legal private school—pay the town the value of the bequest? The question had been raised by a small faction in the town that wanted to force the headmaster to close the school. One member of this group was a woman who had been replaced as school librarian. Another was an artist whose light had been cut off by the shadow of the one dormitory the headmaster had so far succeeded in building. The others were people who resented the growth of the academy in their town and the success of the headmaster, who was not even a native and had become the most powerful man in the valley.

The situation was unpromising. Even when he got successfully past the long legal battle, which he eventually did, the headmaster still had to produce at least a hundred and fifty thousand dollars just to come out even and stay in action for another year. In 1924, that seemed an impossible sum for a country schoolmaster to find. The school would have gone under had it not been for what must surely be one of the most extraordinary gestures in the history of American education. Lewis Perry, headmaster of Exeter, Alfred Stearns, headmaster of Andover, and Horace Taft, headmaster of Taft, left their schools and went to New York and elsewhere to raise money from among their own alumni to save Deerfield. Perry came up with thirty-three thousand dollars in a single day, and within the next five years Perry, Stearns, and Taft raised a million and a half dollars for Deerfield.

Amherst classmates of Boyden's contributed their money and efforts, and so did the presidents of Cornell and Amherst, and Dean Pennypacker of Harvard. "What swayed us was that he had been able to keep that school going with inadequate quarters and salaries," one contributor remembers. "How did he hang on to the teachers? It was a marvel." The headmaster was forty-five in 1924, and his commitment to Deerfield was deeper than he may have realized. "I wasn't as worried as I probably should have been," he says now. Before 1924, according to some long-resident observers in Deerfield, the headmaster was straightforward in his ways, but after he saw what a small concentration of pettiness almost did to his school, he became, as he has remained, a fox.

WHEN THE HEADMASTER had little else to offer, he hung on to his faculty by charming them into a kind of loyal paralysis. Year after year, he promised salary raises and could almost never deliver. As June approached, he would make a modest show of brave loneliness, telling the teachers to move on for their own good, and assuring them that his understanding would be unalloyed with resentment. He said that if, however, they should decide to stay with him, he would never forget it. And he thought that they could all build something together. The faculty, at one time, lived in his house. If

Boyden and his wife wanted to have a private talk, they went down into the cellar and held their conversation behind the furnace. Miss Minnie Hawks sat in a rocking chair in the living room directly overhead, and listened. The headmaster built and has maintained a faculty of solid schoolmen, few of whom have administrative ambitions. Those who do have such ambitions rapidly become headmasters elsewhere. At Deerfield, all ranks between the five-star general and the noncommissioned officers are vacant.

There is a high degree of compatibility between the faculty and the students, partly because they bear an analogous relationship to the headmaster. "I'm not running this school for the faculty," he has often said. "I'm running it for the boys." From early morning until late evening, his faculty's lives must constantly touch the boys' lives—at breakfast, lunch, and dinner, in the classroom, in organized study periods, in club activities, in athletics. The faculty members are expected at all school functions, and there are very few who manage to be simply teachers; most of them have to coach athletic teams and run dormitory corridors as well, not to mention a couple of dozen lesser duties. To some extent this describes all prep-school faculties, but at Exeter and Andover the extent is extremely small, and nowhere is it larger than at Deerfield. The headmaster's idea of a faculty is a group of people who are much in evidence all the time. The faculty is never in a position to complain, because the headmaster and his wife work harder than anyone else at being visible and involved throughout the school day. "The more you coöperate with the headmaster, the more he imposes on you," says a teacher who has been there twenty-five years. "He exacts a fantastic commitment. If you give it, he expects more. If you don't give it, he carries you, but you don't exist." The loyalty of these people sustains the headmaster, and he, in turn, has shown a loyalty to them which has at times seemed foolhardy. He has kept on at the academy men whose deterioration has caused both embarrassment and detriment to the academy but whose earlier contributions helped him build his school. "He has no patience with minor failings, but with big failings he has infinite patience," says an English teacher whose failings, if any, have been minor. Years ago, the same man was offered the post of head of the English department of the Canterbury School, at double his Deerfield salary. "He's not interested in money," said the headmaster, not bothering to compete with Canterbury. The teacher remained at Deerfield. The next year, when he expected a raise, the headmaster passed him over. He has, however, been given a raise in each of the twenty-two other years he has been at the school.

The headmaster's chief disciplinary lieutenant is Donald C. Sullivan, who has been at Deerfield since the nineteen-twenties, and who, in a way, is revered by Deerfield boys for his toughness, probably because of his balancing sense of humor and his apparently perfect sense of what is fair. Years ago, Sullivan, who is known as Red, went after the headmaster in a rage over some now forgotten matter. Seeing the anger in Sullivan's face, the headmaster spoke first. "Let's go into the horse barn, Red. Hurry! I'm hiding from Hen Smith." Hen Smith was one of the town's influential women. In the darkness of the horse barn, the headmaster complained about Hen Smith and how much of his time it took to placate these town women. "Red, I couldn't run this school without you," he slipped in. "Now I'm stuck here, so would you . . ." He sent Sullivan on an errand, and Sullivan didn't realize what had happened until it was much too late to do anything about it.

Deerfield boys have always valued the close relationship that Boyden has effected between the students and the faculty, and they have been conscious of the unusual effort it involves. "I frankly don't understand why any faculty members are at Deerfield," a boy in the class of 1966 said recently. There are two primary reasons. The first, of course, is an appreciation of Boyden and the things he has achieved. "He always stands for and fights for the absolute best," one of his teachers says. "Hence, people go along with him." The second is that the headmaster makes no impositions on the professional style or approach of his teachers in the classroom. "One here has a free hand in the way of teaching his classes; he can try any method he desires and can work in his own way to get results," wrote Tom Ashley in 1916. A teacher who is there now says, "The great thing about Deerfield is that there is no plan book, there are no supervisors, the teachers have freedom."

The headmaster's own talents are extracurricular, and he has always known it. He has never been abreast of new educational ideas, but his wife has always been, and so has his core of first-rate teachers. This is not to say that he ignores Deerfield's academic side. For sixty years or so, until his bad hearing made it impractical, he gave out all grades himself. There were no report cards. Each boy had a private talk with the headmaster six times a year and was told where he stood. In these talks, the headmaster drew the boys out, getting their reactions to their courses, and thus learning where the strength of his faculty was. "Personality counts in teaching at the secondary level," he says. "Personality rubs off. The boys are conscious of meeting a colorful and active mind." Boyden has always had the insight to recognize people like this and the political grip to hold them. Building a group of loyal and talented men is a long process. He has built such a group. Deerfield has a skillful faculty, but not an intellectual one. It includes only one Ph.D. Nonetheless, the school is fairly appraised by a member of the class of 1952, now an editor at a university press, when he says, "The point of a boy's education is to learn to love knowledge. Deerfield gave me that. And I think it developed faster at Deerfield than it would have at most other schools."

In recent years, the headmaster has reacted perhaps

conservatively—and perhaps not—to the great pressure under which contemporary students have to work. The relentlessness of the competition often drops a kind of pall over serious youngsters in high schools and in independent schools, and adjustments have been made in many school programs to reduce non-academic functions, create more time for study, and generally gear up the country's youth for the college-admissions battle. The headmaster believes that this unfortunate intensity erodes four of the better years of a life span, truncates many experiences that are quite possibly of more lasting if less measurable value, and does not necessarily result in better preparation for college. "Work is being crammed down prep schools by colleges," he complains. "We don't set the college-entrance exams. We don't grade them. I don't know what can be done to relieve the pressure under which the boys are working. Frankly, I'm floundering on this." Meanwhile, he has refused to eliminate any of Deerfield's extracurricular activities, from the electronic jazz combo to the Junior C soccer team, or to give up time-consuming traditions, such as Sunday Night Sing and Evening Meeting. He has always thought that four courses were as many as a boy ought to handle, and he will not add a fifth one. The headmaster of another school has said, "Deerfield is not a pressure cooker academically. Most schools are now."

In the college-placement race, all independent schools have lost the sway they once had. Lawrenceville, for example, used to send seventy boys a year to Princeton; there are twelve Lawrenceville graduates in the Princeton class of 1969. Deerfield boys can no longer feel assured about their college choices, either, but the headmaster's refusal to put things on an emergency basis has not cost them their relative position. Numerically, Deerfield is regularly among the top six schools represented in the freshman classes of, for example, Princeton, Harvard, Yale, Dartmouth, and Stanford. Until the early nineteen-sixties, the headmaster made an annual visit to the admissions office at Princeton, where he would be told what Deerfield boys Princeton was about to accept. If the headmaster expressed strong approval of other Deerfield boys whom Princeton had decided to reject, Princeton would change its mind. Boyden was the only man in the country for whom Princeton would do that.

Deerfield is probably the only prep school that has never published a catalogue. "We offer all the courses required by any college or university," the headmaster explains. "A catalogue is expensive. I'd rather give the money as a scholarship to a boy or two. I have never been able to write a catalogue anyway. Those that have been prepared for me I could never live up to. They're idealistic—a sales argument. I don't think we need a sales argument. My successor will publish a catalogue—I'm sure of that."

ADMISSIONS TO DEERFIELD have traditionally been in large part a subjective matter, since the headmaster for years required virtually all applicants to appear for a personal interview and then would rely on his own impressions. If he liked a boy, he would admit him, and then ask the parents what they could pay. This was not a rarity. The academy's treasurers and bookkeepers have never been able to establish a figure for expectable tuition money for an approaching year. He has over a hundred boys there now whose parents have been told to "pay what you can." In 1923, one of his students spent the summer working in Georgia and made two friends whom he thought Deerfield could help. He wrote to the headmaster, who developed an interest and admitted them sight unseen, paying their train fare, forgetting tuition, and buying them second-hand suits when they arrived. In some eras, his admissions policies have seemed a little cranky. He refused to admit English boys for many years, and he went through a period when he was loath to take anyone from Boston. Local girls continued to attend the academy until 1948. Then he closed them out. He discriminates against no one else, including wealthy people, whose money he eagerly seeks, not caring whether it is new, mellowing, or antique. He responds quickly to an applicant who is an athlete. He is also interested in one-year boys, who need either added maturity or extra course-work before going on to college. He has fewer places for them than many schools have, but in the highly organized patterns of Deerfield those who are admitted readily become a part of the whole, and, in some cases, the one year can be as permanently valuable to them as three or four years might have been. Since some of these one-year boys have an embarrassing tendency to score more touchdowns, points, runs, and goals than anybody else, the headmaster has been accused of prejudice in their favor. This was particularly true in 1959 when a boy from the Province of Alberta chose Deerfield instead of the National Hockey League, and, playing for Deerfield, markedly unbalanced all of the games in Deerfield's hockey schedule. The situation, in one sense, was typical. The boy's actual reason for going to Deerfield was to set aside his potentialities in hockey, and, with Deerfield's help, to try for admission to Harvard. He went to Harvard, and was graduated with high honors.

The headmaster will follow his intuition when a situation comes up that appeals to him or seems to hold promise. In September, 1955, he got a telephone call from a boy in Saddlestring, Wyoming, who said that he wanted to go to Deerfield because he wanted to try for Princeton and did not think he was going to make it from Saddlestring. His father, he explained, had refused to underwrite any part of his plan, so he could pay no tuition at all, but he had heard that Mr. Boyden sometimes overlooked tuition, and would he please let him come to the school that fall. School would open in two weeks, and every place was, of course, full. "Oh, sure," said the headmaster. "Come right ahead." The boy eventually did go to Princeton, was elected to Phi Beta Kappa, and became a Rhodes Scholar. Needless to say, the headmaster's impulses have resulted in some spectacular mistakes as well as in dramatic successes. Also, parents have sometimes turned the tables on him with bold gestures of their own. The father of Mutt Ray, the eventual Dartmouth football All-America, was so put out when Deerfield turned down his son that he drove into town with the boy, opened the door of his car, shoved him out, and drove away. Boyden let the boy stay. Mutt Ray is now a trustee of the academy. Another father, refusing to be turned down, drove his twin sons to Deerfield and left them in the headmaster's house. Boyden educated both of them, and one is now his Director of Studies.

Boyden's son John has largely taken over the school's admissions procedures, which are more orderly now than they were in the past. John Boyden points out an interesting parabola in the school's sources of new students. Deerfield started, of course, as a public school, drawing all its students from the valley. By the nineteen-thirties and forties, as many as seventy-five per cent of its students were coming from private pre-prep schools. Deerfield now draws seventy-five per cent from public schools—where, according to John Boyden, most of the better material is.

Before the Second World War, the headmaster all but went to college with his alumni—particularly to Amherst and Williams, which are ten and forty miles, respectively, from Deerfield—and in some cases he lent them money for their college tuition. He would appoint a kind of recording secretary in a group going to any given college, and expect regular reports on everybody's progress. If anything began to go wrong academically, he would send a Deerfield teacher to tutor the deficient alumnus until he was past the crisis. If anything was amiss morally or psychologically, he would go himself, even if he had to travel more than a thousand miles.

Today, the headmaster often gets up before a large group of gray-haired men and begins a talk by saying, "Boys . . ." This happens because men who are today grandfathers, and even great-grandfathers, once sat on the floor at his feet at Evening Meeting. Deerfield has its celebrated and distinguished alumni, but not to an unusual extent, as prep schools go, unless one specifically remembers the fourteen students who were there when the headmaster arrived and then notes among their successors men like the present Governor of Rhode Island, or a Mayo Clinic doctor, or the presidents of Williams, Wesleyan, and Mount Holyoke. What is more interesting is the choice of vocations among Deerfield alumni. There are, of course, more bankers than farmers now; but there are more lawyers than bankers, more doctors than lawyers, and—by a wide margin—more alumni in education than in any other category.

NOTHING ABOUT FRANK BOYDEN lends itself to synopsis, although President Butterfield came close to one when he remarked, "There has to be a strategy as well as an ideal. Only petty people would fail to understand this." Boyden's strategy has sometimes seemed petty, but more often it has seemed inspired. It is best exemplified by his showmanship and his pantoscopic attention to detail. It has been said that a thousand details add up to one impression, and at Deerfield it is the headmaster who adds them up. He thinks in pictures. Once a picture seems right, he wants to keep it that way. Anything that mars it or changes the focus irritates him. To be handed an athletic letter, a citation for academic excellence, or almost any other award, a boy has to walk up onto the stage of the school auditorium: the headmaster stations a teacher beside the steps to see to it that the boy's coat is buttoned. A lengthy and expensively produced concert program once arrived from the printer with one name misspelled. "Miller" had been set as "Millar." The headmaster had the program reprinted. He stages basketball games as if he were the manager of La Scala. Every student has to attend, and all are checked in at the door by masters with clipboards, thus assuring a full house. People come in from all over the valley, too, and the headmaster walks around before the game orchestrating the behavior of his boys, casting acrid glances in the direction of excess commotion, greeting all the farmers, druggists, dentists, and telephone linemen as they come through the door. Then he takes his place on the players' bench. His band, which can compete in blare and grandeur with the bands of the national service academies, fills up the room with things like "The Stars and Stripes Forever" and "Under the Double Eagle" until the color of it all lifts the Deerfield team about a foot and a half off the floor. Deerfield basketball teams play well at home; in fact, some fairly undistinguished ones—middling performers on the road—have gone through an entire season without losing a game there. The headmaster likes the way West Point cadets and Annapolis midshipmen conduct themselves at football games. Deerfield boys march across the campus and down to the lower level to some of their own football games, because the headmaster believes that this expresses loyalty and organization. It is hard to imagine that modern boys would not become cynical about these things, but the level of cynicism among the students at Deerfield appears to be remarkably low. "Much of Deerfield, of course, is a carefully developed image," says one boy who graduated last June. "The headmaster has been meticulous in maintaining this image, and it is the prime ingredient of his success. No matter how much we groaned, we all felt a great deal of pride marching to the football games and saying, in effect, 'This is Deerfield. Try as you will, you'll never beat it.' "

Once, in the nineteen-twenties, when Lewis Perry, of Exeter, made a visit to Deerfield, the headmaster assigned each of a number of boys a pose to strike while Perry walked by; one was to be reading busily at his desk, another browsing through a newspaper in a master's living room, a third straightening his belongings. Some boys had two assignments, in the way that spear carriers disappear from stage one moment and return a bit later as messengers or pages. On athletic trips in the early days, the headmaster had certain handsome specimens get off the bus first, to create the best possible impression. For numerous functions, he has always arranged boys according to height—tall ones in front. He appears to have developed in his mind a picture of a ruddy and athletic fellow whose face somehow spells Deerfield. He places the living approximations of this picture in the front row at church and at Sunday Night Sing, and for many years he formed them into a Dance Committee, which was something like an athletic team with a schedule of girls'-school dances, and, like an athletic team, appeared in a group photograph in the Deerfield yearbook. Supervising the arrangement of boys for other yearbook photographs, he reasoned that the eye goes first to the lower left-hand corner of a picture, so he selected a ruddy and athletic boy to sit in that position. One alumnus says, "We sometimes felt like signed postcards: 'You must come and see our school.'" For a man with so much insight into the needs and thoughts of boys, he has seemed incredibly naïve when he has done some of these things, and it must be said of him that in his drive to buff and shine his developing school he has been utterly unconscious that a few boys might be hurt. Actually, nearly all have been merely amused, if anything. Besides, many of these showmanly wiles have been practiced without the students' awareness.

"Now, boys, we're going to have a lot of visitors this weekend," the headmaster says every week. "If you see people wandering around looking lost, I want you to help them." He stations masters and boys in various places to greet people, and strangers can hardly pass through the town without being stopped, given a tour, and, often, invited to stay for lunch or dinner. "His idea is that if you do anything you do it right—at its best," says Walter Sheehan, headmaster of the Canterbury School, who was once a student and then a master at Deerfield. "Always put yourself out to be courteous, even if it costs a couple of thousand more."

Until 1960, the academy switchboard was in the rear parlor of the headmaster's house. He often sat there and worked it himself. "Hello, Deerfield Academy. . . . One moment, please," he would say, expertly pulling and pushing plugs. For decades, all calls coming into the academy between 10:30 P.M. and 7 A.M. would ring in his bedroom. For a community of about six hundred people, he alone answered the phone in the dead of night. He finally got tired of that four years ago, when he was eighty-two, and hired an answering service. A machine now signs checks for the academy, but until 1960 the headmaster personally signed about six thousand checks a year. At his wedding reception, he fussed because there were no rugs in the school building, and he has been fussing similarly ever since. "If you keep floors and walls nice, it's like having your shoes shined and a clean shirt on," he says. He has been seen mopping floors. He has the gym floor kept like polished brass and classroom floors polished every day. There are no dirty windowpanes. "Bob," he once said to a coach, "I was in your locker room after practice today and there was some tape on the floor."

He is essentially conservative with money, but he will spend any sum to get what he wants. Cut flowers appear regularly in vases all over the campus, and there is a single rosebud on each table in the school store; athletic uniforms are the best available; the dining hall is open all summer, and anyone can eat there; the food served throughout the year is unlimited and excellent; all the school's appointments, from furniture to masonry, are solid, tasteful, and expensive. Most independent schools have business managers. Deerfield, naturally, does not, for such a man would devastate many of the customs established by the headmaster. When people talk to him about economy and hand him charts showing how much more Deerfield spends than other schools, he says that the other schools are not telling the truth. "We can't cut down," he will say. "It would save nothing. By cutting down, we would sacrifice something. The sacrifice would be too great. Deerfield costs money."

The details have long since added up to a place that is incomparably impressive to the eye. Even the grass is a little greener there, growing in fourteen inches of topsoil, and for many years the headmaster went around with a jackknife digging plantain out of his lawns. Last summer, he was riding around in his golf cart one afternoon with his wife and daughter when he saw a mess of papers on the ground. He stopped the cart and sent the two women to pick up the litter. Last fall, an hour or so after the end of a rain-soaked football game, he returned to the field and, until it became too dark to see, moved about alone in the continuing rain, replacing the chunks of turf that had been torn up by the cleats of the players.

T
HE PATTERN OF THE SCHOOL DAY was different
for the headmaster when he was doing a good part of
the teaching, but it has not varied much in the past fifty
years. "You can't stay with him," a member of his faculty remarks. "If you tried to follow him around, he
would have you out cold by four o'clock in the afternoon." He gets up at six, or a little earlier, and while he
is dressing and shaving he frequently prays. It is note-
worthy that he doesn't stop to pray. In the words of one
member of his family, "He goes into nothing without
praying. He prays all the time. He has consummate faith

that the Lord will take care of him." Once, believing himself to be alone, he said to his mirror, "I'm such a God-damned fool." When he saw that one of his children had heard him, he said, "I'm not swearing. I'm praying." Only in rare moments does the headmaster get into a contemplative mood about his work. In one such moment, recently, he said, "I'm not sure, quite seriously, that the Lord didn't put Mrs. Boyden and me here to do this."

At seven, his secretary arrives, and the headmaster is waiting, standing in his study with a Boston newspaper held open at arm's length, so that he is almost completely hidden behind it. He lights a fire. One explanation of his good health may be his use of fire. He is never far from a set of crackling logs. There are fireplaces within five feet of both of his working desks—in his home and in the school building. While he dictates, he sits on the top of the fire screen and bakes himself. There is nothing he likes quite as much as mail. He can't wait to get at it, and it takes precedence over everything else in his routine. He writes thirty-five letters a day, on the average —sometimes as many as seventy—and, as he dictates, he strews the floor with sheets of paper and keeps pitching envelopes into the fireplace. He is not interested in letters that require study, for his batting average has to be maintained. He has developed a kind of X-ray vision. He can stare at a large mound of incoming mail and unfailingly pluck forth the envelopes that contain checks.

He writes mainly to alumni and parents, answering not only their letters but every birth announcement and Christmas card. He answers everything he receives. He acknowledges acknowledgments. If an oil-heater salesman sends him a brochure, he sends off a note saying that he isn't interested. In the past sixty-four years, he has written about five hundred thousand letters, carbons of all of which have been kept in the school-building attic. "He acknowledges trivia sweetly," his present secretary says. And thus he has, in a sense, written his autobiography.

January 25, 1943

Dear Phil:

. . . Foxboro has always meant a great deal to me, and my only regret is that I can't get home more frequently. As I look back, it seems to me that the young people of our time had a very sane, wholesome, active life, and that is just the sort of thing which I have tried to give to the boys at Deerfield.

October 28, 1952

Dear Laura:

Deerfield is a beautiful spot, and since I could not stay in Foxboro I am very thankful to have spent my life here. . . . I remember so well the days in Foxboro and the Sundays when we all went to church, sometimes twice and three times. I also thought of your father as one of the great farmers I have known and your farm as the best in Foxboro.

January 21, 1922

My dear Mr. White:

As you may know, Harvard has been very kind to us, and two or three times it has been insinuated that if we were to throw our influence towards sending boys to Harvard, money might be available. I much prefer, however, to be a free lance, and also to feel that the dominant influence is towards Amherst.

February 28, 1922

Dear Bob:

. . . This letter reminds me of an old lady who used to live with us, and whose tongue ran on forever, and of whom my brother said her only trouble was that she thought out loud. Perhaps you can manage to unravel the two or three points worthwhile.

February 15, 1927

Dear Mr. Reynolds:

I should like to order two suits of the same type and material as my last one. . . .

April 23, 1930

My dear Mr. Stevenson:

Your letter of April 22nd has just been received. Please renew the Full Coverage Insurance on my raccoon overcoat for one whole year.

My dear Mrs. Hammond:

My middle name is an unusual one and quite often
people have asked about it. My father and mother taught
school many years ago in Danvers and lived in the family
of Deacon Learoyd. Although they later returned to Foxboro and my father was in the foundry business, no place
seemed as important in their lives as Danvers. They talked
about it constantly and apparently the happiest years of
their lives were spent there. . . .

He dictates rapidly. At seven-thirty or so, his wife
calls to him from the dining room and tells him that
breakfast is ready. He says, "Just a minute, Helen," and
goes on writing letters. To a guest, he says, "You sit
down and have your breakfast. I'm very sketchy." What
he means by this is soon apparent. A full breakfast has
been prepared—grapefruit, eggs in eggcups, bacon, toast,
and marmalade. The table is handsomely set. He finally
walks in and says hello to his wife in his endlessly imi-
tated voice, which is a sort of light, amiable whine; then
he stands at one corner of the table, picks up a cup, and
drinks hot water. He eats a slice of plain toast. He reaches
into one of his trouser pockets, where he keeps loose
pills like nickels and dimes. He takes out three or four
and swallows them. In twenty seconds, he has had his
breakfast. No root beer and animal crackers this morning. He goes back to work.

February 3, 1928

Dear Charles:

Thank you very much for your cordial invitation to speak before your Men's Club. Unfortunately, I have only one talk, which is the story of the development of Deerfield Academy in general and of Tom Ashley in particular. If you wish me to give that and then answer any questions which may be asked by the men, I shall be glad to do so.

December 10, 1934

My dear Mrs. Graves:

Thank you very much for your cordial invitation to speak for the ladies of the Baptist Church. I am one of the few headmasters who realize their speaking limitations and have not spoken anywhere for the last few years.

September 5, 1953

Dear Mrs. Bannister:

I can come and would be glad to say just a word or two but, as Mrs. Dwight will tell you, I am entirely out of my element. I don't do it well and don't like to do it at all. Mrs. Dwight, as I am sure you know, always speaks well and can talk for an indefinite period.

September 28, 1953

Dear Mr. Cowdrey:

Your letter is a very appealing one and I share your sentiments with regard to Amherst, the Connecticut Valley, and Western Massachusetts. My own home was in the town of Foxboro, but I have been in Deerfield now for fifty-one years and I am thankful to have spent my life in this valley. . . . Many years ago I realized that I was not a good speaker and that that was a field in which I was not qualified and so for many years I have not spoken. I have no definite topic. I would not quite know how to approach any other than an educational subject, and in my work have just gone ahead from day to day without any particular theory or any particular policy except a real personal interest in the boys, in their work, and in their activities. I am afraid you would be very definitely disappointed in any effort which I might make.

September 8, 1949

Dear Mr. Wilk:

I really question the advisability of a moving picture about Deerfield and particularly about me. I hope you will understand, however, how much I appreciate your interest.

June 12, 1948

Dear Mr. Garland:

I have heard several rumors to the effect that I was to retire, but so far as I myself am concerned I have no idea of doing so. . . .

Every secretary he has had remembers this scene: While the headmaster is dictating, his hostler goes by outside the window in the act of exercising one of the headmaster's carriage horses. The headmaster gets up in the middle of a sentence, goes out the front door, and takes over the reins. He rides around in his buggy for ten minutes and comes back, sits up on the fire screen again, and picks up the sentence just where he broke it off. He owns sixteen buggies and four horses. "Nothing will ever take the place of the horse and buggy with me," he says. "I go back to that period. I don't drive much these days, but the mere fact that those horses are out there brings me a lot of comfort." For years after he came to Deerfield, he made his trips home to Foxboro in his buggy—two days, ninety miles, and an overnight in Worcester or Barre. As his children grew up, he often confused their birthdays with the birthdays of colts that had been born at about the same time. His knowledge of the behavior of horses helps him in his handling of boys, and the reverse is probably true as well. The only pilgrimages of any kind that he has ever made have been to Goshen. On the walls of his office in the school building there are, among other things, six pictures of horses, including one of Assault, and a letter from President Eisenhower thanking him for the use of a horse and buggy. Mounted as a hood ornament on the nose tip of Boyden's big black Cadillac is a chromium sulky-and-horse that was given to him by one of his Amherst friends. The car was waiting for the light at Forty-fifth Street and Seventh Avenue one day when a man stepped off the sidewalk, shoved his head through the window,

and—assuming that the headmaster was a trotting king—
asked him for a hot tip on that night's meeting at Roose-
velt Raceway. The headmaster's wife hates horses.

August 23, 1946

Dear Mr. Downing:

Thank you for your letter, which I enjoyed very much.
I wish that more people could experience the thrill of
driving a good horse. Last Wednesday, I drove all three
of mine. The first, Hollywood Robin, was once a very
fast race horse. He has a natural road gait of from ten
to twelve miles an hour. In spite of all his power and
strength, he is very easily handled, and he gets as much
fun out of a trip as I do. Talisman, the second, is a beautiful chestnut with one white ankle and one white leg. He is
a more delicate horse but is very good on the road and in
some ways more of a handful than Robin. Don, the third,
is a fat, lazy, little Morgan who can go just as fast as you
want but will not voluntarily contribute anything to the
speed of the ride. On the other hand, he is a comedian
and keeps the whole stable in an uproar when given the
chance.

October 2, 1953

Dear Mr. Brown:

Yesterday morning early, Bert Tilton, who takes care
of my horses, sent me word that Don was very sick. We
had a veterinary immediately, but there was nothing that
could be done, as he had had a very bad heart attack and
passed away shortly. Up until then, he had been in perfect

health, and just the night before ate his grain and hay and also kicked around because he was feeling so good. I do want you to know how much I have enjoyed him during the twenty-eight years since you sent him down. He has always been very much of a personality, and I have never had a horse that meant so much to me. He liked to travel, and when he couldn't go fast enough to suit himself at a trot would swing into the smoothest pace that I have ever seen any horse have. A ride with him was always a pleasure, because there were always so many exciting things along the road from squirrels to pheasants to attract his attention. There was never anything mean or difficult about him, and everyone, including the little children who came almost every day to see him, will miss him.

December 30, 1953

Dear Mr. and Mrs. Maybury:

Thanks ever so much for your very clever Christmas card. I did not realize that the horse and buggy would be inside the barn until I lifted it up. Those really were good old days, and I wish that more people were in the horse and buggy stage. I am really quite lonesome as I go out, because I guess I am the last one with a driving horse, but I get a real satisfaction as people stop along the street and everyone in the automobiles turns to look at Madagascar as we go along. He really is a wonderful little horse. He is a smart little apple and nothing escapes his attention. Somehow or other, when I get very tired, nothing relaxes or refreshes me so much as to ride behind a good horse.

July 23, 1945

My dear Mr. Hinricks:

I am very much interested in the illustration at the heading of your stationery, for when I first came to Deerfield forty years ago there was an old horse trader with a very long white beard who looked like your illustration. He could drive anything and handle the most difficult horse with no effort whatsoever. I am enclosing a check for $3.00 to cover my subscription to *Hoof Beats*.

Books come and go in the headmaster's study, but some seem to have been there longer than others. Among these are "The Complete Book of Horses," "New Testament in Four Versions," "Herbert H. Lehman and His Era," the *Foundation Directory*, "Ways of Giving to Amherst," "The Reverend Jonathan Ashley House," "Jamestown 1607–1957," *Congressional Directory*, "From Maine Pastures to Vermont Shores," *Miller's Catalog (Everything for the Horseman)*, "Operation Crossroads Africa," "Building a Championship Football Team," "Coaching the Zone and Man-to-Man Pressing Defenses," "Cavalcade of American Horses," "Horses at Home," "Selections from the Old and New Testaments," *Private Independent Schools*, "Steve Mather of the National Parks," "Phillips Exeter Academy—A History." However, the books that the headmaster likes most to read, the novels of Agatha Christie, are not in evidence; he keeps these upstairs. He says that a headmaster does not have time for wide reading, but he has what is known in some circles as the luck of the dip. He can dive into the middle of a book and emerge with a highly quotable fragment that might escape the memory of someone who had read the book thoroughly. A year later, the fragment may pop out in conversation. He is honest about such devices. "You know, I read a very interesting book," he will say, and then he will correct himself, saying, "I didn't actually read the book. I opened it." The magazines in his main living room, strewn about in rampant variety to divert the faculty, include *Defenders of Wild Life News, American Forests,* the *New England Farmer, Main Currents in Modern Thought, Protestant Church Buildings & Equipment, Natural History,* the *United States Investor,* the *National Parks Magazine,* and the *Massachusetts Review* ("New Light on Emily Dickinson").

March 31, 1947

Dear Mr. Sullivan:

I have been away most of the time for the past two weeks and have missed the Foxboro *Reporters* for February twenty-eighth, March eighth, March fifteenth, and March twenty-seventh. If you have any extra copies of those issues, I would appreciate your sending them to me.

October 13, 1934

Dear Mr. Caton:

I saw the other day the notice of your Birthday Anniversary and want to write you and Mrs. Caton a note of congratulation and best wishes. I always remember with pleasure the good times we had at your house and occasionally on Sunday nights my mind goes back to the stereopticon entertainments which you gave at the church.

January 25, 1935

Dear Mr. Finnety:

I was very much interested in the item in the Foxboro *Reporter* about your eighty-eighth birthday. I remember very well when we used to meet at church.

December 16, 1946

Dear Mrs. Thompson:

I have just been reading my copy of the last Foxboro *Reporter* and find that I missed your birthday. I hope that you will excuse me this time and I am putting it down on my calendar for next year.

At nine o'clock, he gives up dictating and goes over to the school building, which he enters through the Browsing Library, a high-ceilinged, oak-panelled room with reference books on its shelves and newspapers on its long oak tables. This morning, a man, a woman, and a boy are standing in one corner, obviously feeling strange as they wait for an interview with a young admissions man. The headmaster walks over to them. "Hello," he says. "My name is Boyden." The people are from Minnesota. The headmaster launches into a long discussion of geographical distribution and its importance to an independent school. Have they, by chance, read the article in the school paper by the boy from Rhodesia? He'll see to it that they get a copy. On he moves into the main corridor, where he meets the admissions director of Rutgers University and the admissions director of Princeton. He tells them a story about a man he recently encountered in a club in New York. The man heard him mention Deerfield, Massachusetts, and said to him, "Do you live there?"

"Yes," said the headmaster.

"Do you know the old man who runs the school there?"

"Yes," said the headmaster.

"How old is he?"

"Eighty-six, I believe."

"Can he still get around?"

A long-distance call comes in from a woman whose son has decided that he wants to go to college immediately and does not want to go through the formality of completing his senior year at Deerfield. The headmaster takes the call at his desk. When he puts the phone down, he sees his athletic director in the corridor and complains to him that there has been a letdown in the way receptions after sports events are handled.

The headmaster of another school—a former master at Deerfield—telephones. "We had them seventeen to fourteen when one of our very good backs fumbled a punt," Boyden tells him. "Andover? They are a little better than Exeter. Playing Exeter was like playing one of our smaller high schools around here. They'll get back at us—don't worry."

He has a call put in for him to Calvin Plimpton, president of Amherst, to whom he complains about a stipulation placed upon Amherst and Deerfield in the transfer of securities from a Wall Street trust to both institutions. "After all," he says, "it was Charlie's money." This is a reference to the late Charles E. Merrill, Amherst '08, a close friend of the headmaster, and a founder of Merrill Lynch, Pierce, Fenner & (in his time) Beane.

"There is nothing like giving money away," Merrill once said happily to the headmaster.

"Charlie," said the headmaster, "we see eye to eye."

He sits down at his desk to watch the boys go by between classes. He waves to them and calls two aside to ask them questions. When the building has become quiet again, he goes downstairs and into the duplicating room, where he fusses with some papers and makes unflattering remarks about the Xerox machine, not because it jams once in a while but because it is a machine. He goes into another room and tells the alumni secretary about a trip he made to New York the previous day. (An observer standing outside 30 Rockefeller Plaza might have seen him step out of the car in a cold wind, without his coat, slightly stooped, and with a frayed briefcase under his arm. He handed the doorman a dime and moved toward the revolving door of the great skyscraper, looking very worn and tired. Anyone's heart would have gone out to him for undertaking these long, exhausting journeys for his school, going alone to make rounds of the city that would last all day. But the pathos of it all was modified, because when he came back out through that revolving door he had a hundred thousand dollars in the briefcase.) He reports this sum to the alumni secretary. "I just look old and frail and sick," he once told a Deerfield parent in describing his approach to fund-raising. Throughout his career, he has assiduously cultivated the appearance of helplessness—a talent for which he has found many practical applications.

He talks to the master who runs the school bookstore about remodeling the store and doubling its size. The downstairs corridor is jammed with teachers drinking coffee. He talks to one after another—thirty seconds apiece. He retreats to a small room to discuss ideas for a new library with his faculty committee on architecture, which includes his son John. He goes back up to the main floor and stops to speak to a boy from India who is about to be interviewed by the man from Princeton. Another headmaster is on the phone—like the earlier caller, a former master at Deerfield. He has lost a physics teacher and needs one as soon as possible. Boyden says he will do what he can. He spends a few moments with the admissions man from Swarthmore. He signs a couple of dozen letters. His handwriting is firm and forthright, unflorid but remarkably graceful. Penmanship like his has not been widely taught or practiced in this century. For ten minutes, he confers with a fellow-trustee of the University of Massachusetts, who has stopped in on his way through town. The headmaster is chairman of the university board. The University of Massachusetts was once the Massachusetts Agricultural College, a small institution in Amherst. It had a thousand students in the early nineteen-fifties, and, like all state schools in Massachusetts, it was under complete legislative control. The college couldn't make a move—could not even hire a new teacher or schedule a new course—without the approval of the state. Boyden eventually changed that. In 1962, he persuaded the legislature to give autonomy to the university. The university has increased its enrollment to over thirteen thousand, and in a few years it will level out at twenty thousand. New buildings—some by I. M. Pei, Marcel Breuer, Kevin Roche, and Edward Durell Stone—radiate from the original campus not so much by the dozen as by the mile. One new building, the largest gymnasium in the United States, is called the Frank L. Boyden Physical Education Building. Boyden has presided over all this development with a hand that is used to holding reins. He is known among his fellow-trustees, many of whom come from the eastern part of the state, as "the fastest gavel in the west."

The headmaster says goodbye to his fellow-trustee at the Browsing Library door, then, within eight minutes, talks with an alumnus who has brought his son to the school as a candidate for admission; a boy who has just been interviewed by Harvard; another alumnus and his wife; and a master who is eager to tell him—and is given sixty seconds to do so—that a visitor from Groton was impressed by Deerfield's new dormitories. Still another applicant for admission comes into the school building with his father. The headmaster urges the father to sit down and talk, while the boy is interviewed elsewhere. The headmaster's treatment of the man is too excited for this to be, say, the president of Bethlehem Steel, so he must have something to do with a major-league baseball club. The man actually owns one. The headmaster apologizes that he is no longer coaching at Deerfield and starts to talk about Leo Durocher and Warren Spahn. The conversation lasts for more than half an hour and never once touches upon the man's purpose in coming to Deerfield, but his son's chances of getting in are one-in-one. After they leave, the headmaster reviews the afternoon schedule, talks for several minutes with a math teacher, goes into a study hall and touches the arm of a sleeping boy, returns to his desk, signs more letters, and tells another story to the admissions man from Princeton.

It is almost noon. He goes over to his house for a short nap. He is not taking the nap because he is eighty-six and needs it in order to keep going. He has been doing this all his life. Even more than fireplace fires, his naps are the essence of his mechanism, for he can go to sleep absolutely anywhere, at any time, and he can sleep soundly, if he chooses, for less than three minutes. Sometimes, while he is interviewing parents, he will press a button and his secretary will appear and say that he has a phone call. Excusing himself, he goes out, holding up five fingers to indicate the number of minutes he wants to sleep. He pulls a shawl over himself. It takes him thirty seconds to fade out. After five minutes, he is awakened. Up goes the hand again, this time with three fingers extended. Three minutes later, the secretary awakens him again. He gets up—as fresh as if he had slept through a night—and goes back to the interview. The first component of this art is that he can wash his mind free of anything at any time. Then he starts at the north end of the village and tries to remember who lives in the first house. George Lunt. Then he moves to the next house. He has never got beyond the third house. He can go to sleep while he is waiting for an operator to put through a call. Most of the time on automobile trips, he either dictates or sleeps. On athletic trips with his teams, when he was the coach, he used to sleep all the way, and the only things that could wake him up were "kid stuff," as he would put it, or off-color stories. "Cut that out," he would say, and go back to sleep.

The headmaster wakes up from his midday nap and decides to take a quick look around the school before lunch. He believes correctly that the more people see of him—students and faculty alike—the more smoothly his school will run. "You won't see any confusion anywhere, I'm sure," he says. (Recently, he was scheduled to go on a complicated journey from Deerfield to Worcester to Chicago and back to Deerfield. He went to Worcester but decided to backtrack to Deerfield. It was 5 P.M. when he reached the campus, and at that time the greatest concentration of students happened to be in the gymnasium. He walked into the gym, stayed two minutes, walked out of the building, and went on to Chicago.) Getting into his golf cart, he shoots at full throttle along Albany Road, which goes through the center of the campus and forms a right angle with the long town street. He loops, twists, drives with his hands off the wheel, dives downhill, shaves trees, goes up the left side of the street into oncoming traffic, and waves and honks to people without regard to obstacles rapidly approaching. He has never actually known how to drive a car, but he used to swirl around Deerfield in an old Pontiac he had, going everywhere at top speed in second gear, because that was the only gear he knew how to find. People learned to get out of his way then. Today, although the golf cart is less alarming, everyone remains alert. He goes out onto his baseball field, spins around second base, and looks back at the academy. "Let's not be boastful, but let's be thankful for what we've got," he says. "Isn't it beautiful? We didn't have anything for so long that we had years and years to think of what we would like. I go around as often as I can to make sure it's still there. This is the kind of day when you get the shadows on the hills and the mist on the river. I've been so fortunate all my life to live in the country."

He sees the coach of Junior A soccer and drives about three hundred yards to intercept him and tell him how he wants the reception after the Junior A soccer game a few hours hence to be run. "I like receptions run better than they have been this fall," he says. "I don't like boys getting loose in the store and then wandering into receptions with ice-cream cones." He drives over to the Memorial Building, where the reception will be held, for he wants to make sure that everything has been properly set out. Before he goes in, he removes the keys to the golf cart and puts them into his pocket. On his way out, he wipes a bit of dust off a windowsill. He goes to the gymnasium and downstairs to the football locker room, where he weighs himself. One hundred and forty-four. He is pleased. He notices the blackboard: "BEAT WORCESTER—THEY'LL BE TOUGHER THIS YEAR." "That's high-school stuff," he says, and he erases the sentiment from the board. On the front steps of the gym, he picks up a crushed, lipstick-smeared cigarette butt and carries it back into the building as if it were a dead rat. He puts it in a wastebasket, straightens a bench, and goes home to have lunch with his wife.

After another nap, he gives an hour-long tour of the school to an alumnus from Michigan who has returned, with his wife and son, after a long absence. Then he gets into his Cadillac and departs for Amherst, where he has an appointment. The car is driven by Foster F. Babinèau, who is known as Fuzzy and is in his late fifties. Fuzzy's predecessor in the job was his father-in-law. On major highways, the headmaster sometimes gets out a stopwatch and times Fuzzy as he sails past the mileposts. If his calculations don't please him, he tells Fuzzy to speed it up. In twenty-three years, the headmaster has never told Fuzzy to slow down. "And, boy," says Fuzzy, "have we had some pretty good rides!" The headmaster will get into the car in Deerfield and tell Fuzzy what time he has to be where. Then it is up to Fuzzy to get him there, even if the destination happens to be more miles away than there are minutes left before the appointment. It was the same way with Fuzzy's father-in-law. In those days, the headmaster often used a train called the Minute Man for his longer trips, but, of course, he had to catch it. The Minute Man's route went along the base of the hills to the west of the school, across the river. The headmaster would wait until it went by, then go out and jump in the car and tell Fuzzy's father-in-law to go after it. Sometimes they caught the train at the next stop, sometimes two stops down the line, but it never got away. The night of the Brink's robbery, in 1950, a squadron of state policemen closed in on the Cadillac, waved Fuzzy over, and told him to get out, because they were going to investigate the car. The headmaster was asleep, but he sat up and said, "Tell them to go away." They went away. Fuzzy spends more time with the headmaster than anyone else does. "He's never given me hell for anything," Fuzzy says. "If that isn't a record, I don't know. God knows he could have. You know, weather has never questioned that man. We've left Deerfield in blizzards. He's a corker. He's drier than a covered bridge."

The headmaster's appointment is at Amherst's new Robert Frost Library, where he has asked Deerfield's architect, William Platt, to meet him and talk about Deerfield's new library, which will incorporate similar features. He points out to the architect what an exciting opportunity this is to create something unparalleled among facilities at secondary schools. Then he tells the architect exactly how he wants each element to be done. He returns to Deerfield and has dinner with three young admissions men from Harvard. He reminisces about his friend Dean Pennypacker, their distinguished predecessor, who died before they were born.

At half past six, the faculty fills up the headmaster's living room, having after-dinner coffee. On some occasions during this daily event, the headmaster has clapped his hands and told everyone to be sure to go to the town hall and vote on zoning, or a bond issue, or whatever happens to be going on in politics in the valley. If the headmaster is an educator by intuition, he is a politician by instinct. While he was building his school, he built

[103]

himself into a political force incomparably more powerful than the headmaster of any school would be simply
by virtue of his position. Boyden started by going around
to church suppers all over the area. He served for
years as town constable; he represented the district at
state conventions; and he opened up his academy for the
use of the community. Every three or four weeks, for
decades, a banquet has been held there for hundreds of
people—Red Cross, county assessors, Community Fund,
a tool company's annual blast. The headmaster charges
little or nothing. Once a month, the village Men's Club
eats gluttonous slabs of roast beef for fifty cents apiece.
At Commencement time, the great academy dinner is
open to anyone from anywhere, and hundreds of people
come. The headmaster is paying them back. When he
had no money, the great academy dinner was prepared
by farmers' wives, who brought the food with them.
During the First World War, the academy boys saved
local businessmen by unloading freight cars, and throughout the Second World War they picked potatoes. The
headmaster constantly repeats to his boys the theme of
responsibility to the community, of the need for all of
them to become engaged citizens. From this base he has
risen to be "the master politician in western Massachusetts," as one man in Greenfield puts it, going on to say,
"All people in this part of the state consult him when
they are thinking of running for office." A Massachusetts
state policeman once said, "The headmaster is the only

person of importance around here who calls us all by our first names." In 1959, when Nelson Rockefeller was trying to decide whether to seek the Republican nomination for President, he invited ten men from New England to a meeting in New York. Boyden was one of the ten—and not because Rockefeller had earlier sent two sons to Deerfield. The will of Charles Merrill was a complicated one—it involved payments to Deerfield, Amherst, and other institutions, spread out over many years—and a tax ruling was made that was unfavorable to the beneficiaries. They stood to lose millions, and the only way to change the situation was through an Act of Congress. The possibility of such legislation was considered nil by everyone but the headmaster, so one day in 1957 Boyden went alone to Washington. He was there only long enough to look up his contacts in Congress, the Senate, the Cabinet, and the White House. The bill was written and passed. The headmaster recently moved a proposed alignment for an interstate highway with a flick of his elbow. No one knows the number of people in the valley who are wholly or partly supported by him, but no one doubts that it is considerable. His charitable instincts have never been reckless, however. In 1940, a man in Greenfield wrote to the headmaster, told him that he was out of money, winter was coming, his children were sick, and he would be immeasurably grateful if the headmaster could send him two tons of coal. The headmaster sent him one ton of coal.

September 29, 1955

Dear Sherm:

I am sorry about the President's Birthday Party, for we had such a good time at the one in Pennsylvania.

February 7, 1959

Dear President Eisenhower:

Thank you for your letter. As always I am very grateful to you for the appointment to the Jamestown-Williamsburg-Yorktown Celebration Commission. . . . I think back with much pleasure to the half-hour which you gave me when you took one minute to say you could not come to Deerfield and then suggested that since we had twenty-nine minutes left we talk about something in which we were both interested and experienced—namely, the seventeen to eighteen year old boy. I was also very glad that you and Mrs. Eisenhower used my cart for the Birthday Celebration in Hershey.

September 24, 1957

Dear Nelson:

This is a letter which does not require an answer, but I did want to tell you how interested I am in your efforts to keep the Dodgers in Brooklyn.

December 15, 1923

Dear Father Sullivan:

I have just been looking at the Greenfield *Recorder* for December 8th, and have seen the notice of your ordination to the priesthood. Please accept my hearty congratulations on the completion of your studies. I am always very much interested in the progress of any of the boys from this section with whom I have been associated in athletics and otherwise. I always felt during your connection with the high school in Turners Falls that you had real power of leadership.

Tonight, in place of the ordinary Evening Meeting, a visiting alumnus is going to describe to the boys his experiences swimming under the ice in the Antarctic and recording the sounds of seals. The headmaster talks first, telling the boys how nice it is to have alumni return, especially from such remote and unusual places, and as he goes on in this vein he is before his school in his most characteristic attitude. He has gripped both lapels of his double-breasted jacket, and he draws them together as if he were cold. He wrinkles his nose. He has a smile on his face, and he interrupts himself with soft, inaudible laughter. He sits down to hear the lecture, resting one ankle on the other knee.

After the evening study period, the headmaster's living room fills up again—this time with varsity athletes, who have come for milk, crackers, and a blackboard talk by the coach. The coach is modern, very able, and technical. The headmaster adds a few words that are not even faintly technical. These brief evening gatherings of football, basketball, and baseball players have been going on at the headmaster's house for about fifty years. When the boys have gone, he sits down, puts his ankle up on his knee, and says, "I don't feel any less power or any less vigor than I did forty years ago. I'm hoping to be able to have three more years."

In the late nineteen-thirties, some prospective Deerfield parents hesitated before sending their sons to Deerfield because they thought that the headmaster, being close to sixty, might be nearing the end of his career. Among these was Henry N. Flynt, who did decide to send his son to Deerfield and is now the chairman of the academy's board of trustees and the head of the foundation that has financed the preservation of many Deerfield houses. The headmaster himself, in the nineteen-thirties, said to a member of his faculty, "One of the things I regret is that I am not going to live long enough to see how Deerfield boys do." In the mid-forties, the headmaster began saying, "If I can only have five more years . . ."—a stock preamble to a discussion of his plans of the moment. He used this same line through the nineteen-fifties and the early sixties. Now, in his living room, he repeats, "I'm hoping to be able to have three more years. I'd like five, but I'm very conscious of my age. Look, I'm not selfish about it. I'm not going to bother anybody by hanging on too long, but I would like to see the library finished. Perhaps I will have to retire someday, but I'm not setting any definite date."

The headmaster recently wrote a long, discursive letter to all Deerfield alumni and parents in which he obscurely used the word "retire." Hundreds of eloquent testimonials and thousands of dollars arrived by return mail. Answering the letters, he thanked everyone and assured them that he had no intention whatever of retiring. "I've got to do an awful lot in three years, if I can," he says. "I have a feeling that if you've got something good enough to be preserved, it will be. I just kept working. I have never had time enough to concentrate on any one difficulty. The thing I have tried to build is a unity of feeling. The thing I hope is always retained here is the school's flexibility. We've just kept abreast of the times. We haven't gone wild. There's a sense of permanence in the school."

He looks with surprise at some notes about the academy that were written by him in 1906. They have been filed away for sixty years, and he has forgotten that they existed. "The object of the school should be the development of character, to help each pupil to do that for which he is best suited," he reads. "This can be done in the country, because the comparatively small numbers make it possible to do much personal work, and the relationship between pupil and teacher becomes more intimate."

"Not bad," he says. "I was ahead of things, wasn't I? I didn't know I could do it."

Photographs

*Deerfield, Massachusetts, in 1902, was essentially one street
—a mile from the north to the south end—under shade so
deep that even in the middle of the day the braided tracery
of wagon ruts became lost in shadow a hundred yards from
an observer.*

It would be difficult to imagine a more beautiful setting for a school or a more attractive school in the setting. This is the center of the Deerfield campus, as it is today.

When Frank L. Boyden first saw Deerfield Academy, this is what he saw—a dispiriting red brick building that appeared to have been designed to exclude as much sunlight as possible, and a student body of fourteen boys and girls.

[114]

The *1911 Deerfield baseball team. Upper right: Frank L. Boyden, headmaster, coach, first baseman. Third from left, front row: Captain Tom Ashley.*

He believed in wearing the boys out. They dug ditches; they also made beehives, incubators, and wheelbarrows; and, with axes and crosscut saws, they cut lumber for lockers for their athletic equipment. The boy at the far right of the photograph is Tom Ashley.

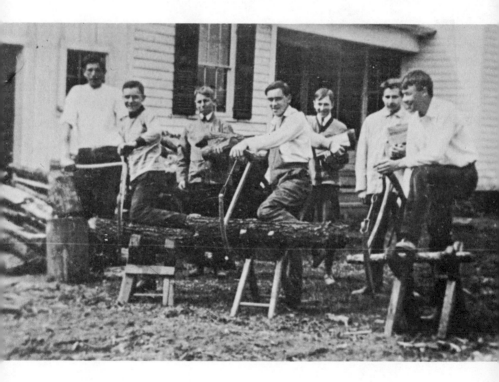

Tom Ashley

In his early years in Deerfield, the headmaster frequently went out into the fields of the surrounding Pocumtuck Valley in a borrowed horse and buggy and talked to young farm boys until he had persuaded them to go to school. This picture was taken in 1953. The fields are much the same, but the boys could be from Michigan, Maine, or Wyoming.

At the age of twenty-two, the new headmaster looked forbidding but hardly forceful.

At the age of four, when he was a member of what he
has described as "a tough Sunday school class," he had a
kind of reinforced gravity in his eyes which suggested that
if this little boy were to clap his hands everyone within earshot would fall silent.

The headmaster's father, Benjamin Franklin Boyden, has been remembered as a bit of a Micawber with a gift for words.

"My mother was quiet, and a very good Sunday school teacher. She was a gracious and devout religious person."

Two men who gave the headmaster aid and encouragement when he was in particular need of aid and encouragement were Lewis Perry (right), headmaster of Exeter, and John Winant (standing), who was Governor of New Hampshire in the late nineteen-twenties and early nineteen-thirties and Ambassador to the Court of St. James's during the Second World War. This picture was taken in the nineteen-twenties.

In his first year at Deerfield, he set up a card table beside a radiator just inside the front door of the school building. This was his office, not because there was no room for a headmaster's office anywhere else but because he wanted nothing to go on in the school without his being in the middle of it. Years later, when the present main school building was built, the headmaster had the architect design a wide place in the first-floor central hallway—the spot with the heaviest traffic in the school—and that was where his desk was put and where it still is.

He has a remarkable eye for trouble. If the mood of the student body at large is poor, he will sense it, and when one boy is disturbed, he will see it in the boy's face, and he will think of some minor matter they need to talk over, so that he can find out what the difficulty is and try to do something about it.

"*You must have your boys together as a unit at least once a day, just as you have your family together once a day.*"

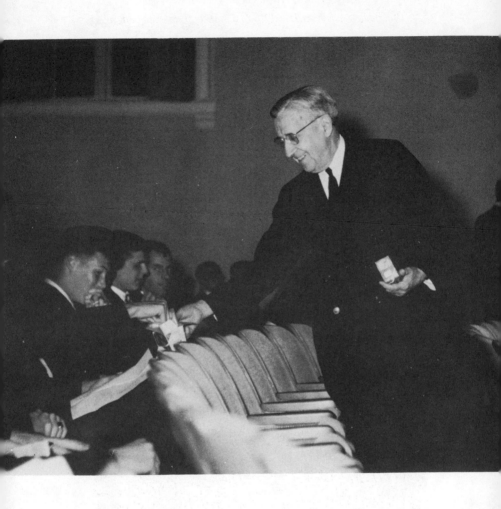

Animal crackers.

For about sixty years, students at Deerfield have referred to the headmaster as the Quid, a name that evolved in an era when Deerfield boys chewed tobacco. If the headmaster approached when they were chewing, whoever saw him first would say "quid" to the others, and everyone would attempt to hide his quid. In more recent times, the headmaster's long black limousine has frequently been referred to as the Quidillac.

He is never far from a set of crackling logs. He dictates every morning, usually from seven until nine.

During the Second World War, Deerfield boys helped local farmers by picking potatoes. The headmaster was there to see to it that no one's patriotism declined.

His sense of football has always been vague but imaginative.
His blocking assignments were not precise. During his years
as player-coach, he put straps on the belts of his linemen so
that the backs—himself included—could hang on and be
pulled forward for short gains.

He continued to hit fungoes to his baseball teams until he was seventy-five years old. It was a high point of any Deerfield baseball day to watch him hit precise grounders to his scrambling infield.

His main talent as a coach was that he always seemed to know what a boy could do and then expected no more of him.

"She is much more important than I am. She has a wonderful sense of humor and deep affection for the boys. She has more influence on the boys than I have. She makes them want to do the work. Her judgment is excellent. She could have been the head of any school."

She is gentle, understanding, forgiving, irreverent about her husband. Beyond this, she is the brightest person on the faculty and the busiest employee of the school.

Smith College once gave Mrs. Boyden an honorary degree with a citation that read: "To Helen C. Boyden, who, with some small help from her husband, built a great school."

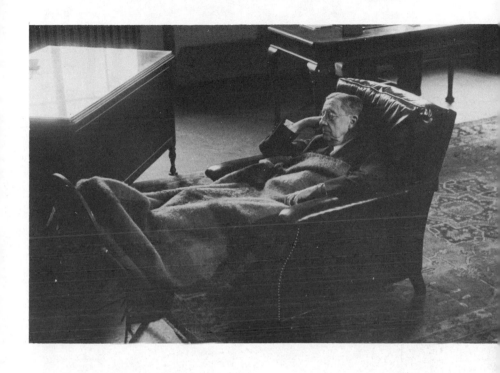

PHOTO CREDITS